how to talk to your kids About Sexuality

By **David L. Scherrer**
and **Linda M. Klepacki**

Building the New Generation of Believers

An Imprint of Cook Communications Ministries
COLORADO SPRINGS, COLORADO • PARIS, ONTARIO
KINGSWAY COMMUNICATIONS, LTD., EASTBOURNE, ENGLAND

NexGen® is an imprint of
Cook Communications Ministries, Colorado Springs, CO 80918
Cook Communications, Paris, Ontario
Kingsway Communications, Eastbourne, England

HOW TO TALK TO YOUR KIDS ABOUT SEXUALITY
©Copyright by David L. Scherrer and Linda M. Klepacki

First printing 2004
Printed in the United States.
 2 3 4 5 6 7 8 9 10 08 07 06 05

Editor: Susan Martins Miller
Cover and Interior Design: Dana Sherrer, iDesignEtc.
Interior illustrations: Ron Adair
Cover photo: © Getty Images

Dedication

I dedicate this book to Norris and Lila Scherrer, my dad and mom.
Thank you for modeling God's love, wedded faithfulness,
a consistent ethic of hard work, courage through trials and
a sense of humor. I love you.

David

With love and honor to my mom and dad,
Cecelia and Bob Larson.
Thank you for parenting me within a loving family
and the knowledge of God our Father.

Linda

Contents

Introduction

There is more to sex than skin to skin. Sex is as much a spiritual mystery as physical fact. As written in Scripture, "The two shall become one ...." We must not pursue the kind of sex that avoids commitment and intimacy, leaving us lonelier than ever—the kind of sex that can never "become one." There is a sense in which sexual sins are different from all others. In sexual sin we violate the sacredness of our own bodies, those bodies that were made for God-given and God-modeled love, for "becoming one" with another (1 Corinthians 6:16–18, *The Message*).

What an awesome time in history to be living and raising a family! Technology makes our lives easier and more flexible than ever. Because we can access information from most anywhere in the world, living and working wherever we want is within reach. Information on most any subject is just a click away. But our non-stop ride on the information highway is changing our culture in one generation. It is awesome and frightening at the same time.

The values and morals that parents have carefully passed from generation to generation are being replaced by pop-culture values that kids access in an instant. Well-meaning kids find themselves constantly bombarded by the lies of post-modern society. The implications for parents are staggering. What are we to say and do as our children approach their teen years and we realize that we're going to have to deal with the fact that they're sexual beings?

Instead, speaking the truth in love, we will in all things grow up into him who is the Head, that is, Christ (Ephesians 4:15).

These are action words! Scripture urges us to speak in love so that all of us will grow to be more like Christ. We have to be more active than ever in our children's lives. We must listen, speak and follow up every day, with every chance we get.

We start this process of speaking truth when our children are just beginning to talk and understand. We speak truth about right and wrong when our children are young. It's really clear to children that running across a four-lane road is dangerous. Why? Because the first time we see them start across the road we turn beet red, scream and grab them by the arm and pull them back to our side. It's clear to them what we mean—under no circumstances are they to do that again!

But what about when it comes to seeing our children grow into their sexuality? This is not the time to get tongue-tied! But for most parents, the approach of puberty kicks off a three-step process:

Step 1: Avoid seeing this happen for as long as we can.
Step 2: Search for all the information on the planet we can find regarding every possible aspect of human sexuality.
Step 3: Repeat Step 1, big time!

Let's begin a journey together to change that three-step process. We'll explore some of the most important issues in our kids' lives. We'll look at sexual influences in the world today and the consequences they bring.

> *So we fix our eyes not on what is seen, but on what is unseen. For what is seen is temporary, but what is unseen is eternal* (2 Corinthians 4:18).

Most of us desperately want our children to have the love of Christ in their hearts and the power and character to live in that love. Things unseen. Can we help our kids receive those gifts? You bet! How? With love. And love in the language of youth is spelled T-I-M-E. We must spend time with our kids in their world. That means doing what they want to do when they want to do it. There's no other way to truly know them. They're changing into adults. No matter how foreign their world seems, we need to plunge in and learn to relate to their emerging adulthood.

What that means for many of us is sleepless nights. That's because the prime time for kids to talk about sex and relationships is after midnight. Why is that? Who knows? It's just one of those weird facts. It may cost us some droopy mornings to talk to them when they're ready. But being available in the wee hours means we have access to open hearts and teachable moments. It may be the most important investment of time we ever make.

A key part of building strong relationships with our emerging teen-adults is to communicate God's beautiful design for sexuality. This book will not run from tough subjects. In a world that delivers a stream of deadly lies, kids need God's undiluted truth. They deserve straightforward answers to their tough questions. And they deserve parents, teachers, coaches and pastors who will be their fiercest advocates. That means clearly communicating the non-negotiables in God's Word. And that's what this book is all about.

God designed sex for the marriage partnership.

Scripture calls sex outside of marriage fornication. For married people, sex with someone other than your spouse is adultery. This behavior is condemned as unholy, unrighteousness, impure and immoral. See Exodus 20:14; Matthew 15:19; and 1 Corinthians 6:9–20.

God condemns deviant sexual behavior.

Deviant sexual behavior, including homosexuality, bestiality, incest and pedophilia, is prohibited in Scripture. In our current society much of this behavior is condoned. Sometimes Christians are called unloving or discriminatory for believing otherwise. But God's definitions of right and wrong are crystal clear. It's tough for both kids and adults to stand on God's truth in a culture steeped in relativism. See 1 Corinthians 6:9, 10; Leviticus 18:21–23; and 1 Corinthians 5:1, 2.

God designed sex to be a beautiful expression of love between a husband and a wife.

The Song of Solomon is an allegory of tender, passionate love that is neither dirty nor embarrassing to the author. This allegory continues in the New Testament as Christ describes himself as the groom and the church as his bride. Just as we, the church, are to be for God alone, so husbands and wives are to be devoted to each other. When we engage in sex outside of God's plan, we tarnish the image and character of God for our partner and ourselves. See Song of Solomon and John 3:29.

God is full of mercy and grace.

Every good thing designed by God can be destroyed and perverted. This is the result of sin, and the payment is death. But God has shown his great love for us by providing his Son as a ransom for our sin, even the sin of sexual immorality. In his Son, we are seen as holy and righteous regardless of our past. What great news! See Matthew 6:14, 15; Mark 11:25; and 1 John 1:8, 9, 4:10.

Wouldn't it be great if we could do everything perfectly from the get-go? Unfortunately, that's not an option. We live in a world that's tainted by sin. Our mistakes, whether purposeful and inadvertent, bring harm to ourselves and others. Sin came into the world when Adam and Eve chose to disobey God in the Garden of Eden (Genesis 3). Since then, every mistake represents a landmine; every step we take is a dangerous venture.

But the truth of God's Word changes our lives. It sets us free! God's Word gives us a map that shows us how to avoid the land mines. This book is designed to help you lay God's road map for sexuality before your young adult. This precious knowledge will give kids confidence to negotiate the pressures of a twisted society, and the courage to invite others to come along. Your child needs this knowledge to survive!

What to Expect

Some books are calming and reflective. They beckon you to snuggle up with a cup of hot chocolate and be comforted. This is *not* one of those books. This book grabs you by the lapels and makes you confront life and death situations with fear and trembling.

If you are studying this book with a group of parents, you'll get the most out of discussion if you've read the chapters ahead of time. You'll be ready to help others and receive help. Others in your discussion group will be at different places in their life journeys. Some may be desperate for answers; others may just be looking for emotional support. Some may have a child just entering puberty and are scared; others may have three teenagers and are terrified! You will feel most comfortable sharing and listening if you approach these topics with an open heart. Bear in mind that you are seeking God's wisdom together, wisdom God has promised to give us. God may speak to you through the reflections of someone in your group. A leader's guide at the back of the book will help guide your discussions.

If you're reading this book on your own, talk to yourself! You may be tempted to breeze through the questions. If you just have to breeze through something, breeze through the sports page or skim the TV section, not this! Prayerfully reflect on each question. Be open to the guidance of the Holy Spirit. He wants to have a conversation with you. Take the time to write your feelings and thoughts in the spaces provided. Read the leader's guide at the back of the book and accept the "prayer and dare" challenges for each chapter. As the saying goes:

If we always do what we have always done,
we will always get what we always got!

We don't want to settle for second or third best for our children. We want God's very best for them. That is what this study is all about—life and love at its best, blessed and protected by God.

chapter one

IT'S TIME TO Talk

Maybe you've seen or heard a conversation something like this:

"You see, son, when you get older and fall in love. And then...uh...you see...uh...if you fall in love enough...well, then uh...it happens that...uh...First you get married!...uh...that is real important...and uh...if you are married long enough and stay in love...not that your mom and I aren't in love, you see...uh...well then...you see...uh...babies happen!...Do you get what I am talking about here, son?"

"Dad, are you trying to talk about getting pregnant and babies? We learned about that in school in fifth grade."

"That's right, son, that's right. I knew that. I just wanted to make sure you understood. I am proud of you, son. Now let's go get that ice cream I was promising. I'm sure glad we had that little chat...why...I can remember when I was young back on the farm when my dad..."

This is the general impression of parental sex education. Not too flattering, is it? But that "birds and bees" talk hasn't improved much over the years. And it's so easy to let the TV or movies do the talking for us...but that's a big mistake! Parents are to be the primary sex educators of their children. There is no Plan B for those of us in God's family.

Teaching values and godly character isn't a one-time event. It is not the "big talk." It is a lifestyle of modeling and mentoring. It starts at birth, when you hold your child for the first time and begin establishing an environment of love and trust.

As our kids grow, we work hard to understand them and meet their needs. We treat them as individuals. After all, no one knows our children like we do. So when the topic of sex comes up, we need to be prepared to be more than age-appropriate. We have to be person-appropriate.

Fifth graders are different than teens. And a 13 year old is light years away from a 19 year old. We need to access all the grace and wisdom God has promised us to stay current and to help shape our children into responsible, self controlled young adults.

MENTORING SPELLED W.I.T.H.

Modeling and mentoring requires you to be *with* your kids. Let's see what that looks like and what kinds of results you can expect. We'll take our example from a couple of guys in Jerusalem around 34 A.D.

Peter and John caused a major stir when they healed the man at the temple. The temple leaders had them arrested when they took the opportunity to preach to the gathering crowd. After spending the night in jail, Peter and John were brought before the Sanhedrin, where they proceeded to blow the Jewish scholars away with their knowledge, courage and authority. Let's look at it straight from Scripture.

> *The next day the rulers, elders and teachers of the law met in Jerusalem. Annas the high priest was there, and so were Caiaphas, John, Alexander and the other men of the high priest's family. They had Peter and John brought before them and began to question them: "By what power or what name did you do this?"*
>
> *Then Peter, filled with the Holy Spirit, said to them: "Rulers and elders of the people! If we are being called to account today for an act of kindness shown to a cripple and are asked how he was healed, then know this, you and all the people of Israel: It is by the name of Jesus*

*Christ of Nazareth, whom you crucified but whom God raised from
the dead, that this man stands before you healed. He is "the stone
you builders rejected, which has become the capstone. Salvation is
found in no one else, for there is no other name under heaven given
to men by which we must be saved."*

*When they saw the courage of Peter and John and realized that they
were unschooled, ordinary men, they were astonished and they took
note that these men had been with Jesus!* (Acts 4:5–15)

MENTORING. IT'S THE LATEST THING! OR IS IT?

Two thousand years ago, Jesus knew that courage, faith, discipline,
diligence, prayerfulness and obedience are *caught,* not *taught!* He knew
the disciples would face stiff challenges, so he wouldn't settle for any
training but the best. His plan was straightforward and simple. Follow
me. Be with me. Pay attention! No seminars or power lunches, no
distance learning environments or video conferencing for Jesus. His
was a ministry of hanging around! Luke 8:1 notes, "After this, Jesus
traveled about from one town and village to another, proclaiming the
good news of the kingdom of God. The Twelve were *with* him." In Mark
3:7, "Jesus withdrew *with* his disciples to the lake, and a large crowd
from Galilee followed." Over and over to those who would listen he
said, "*Follow* me." Some listened and obeyed, most found excuses.

The disciples sat, studied and traveled *with Jesus,* sinners ate and
fellowshiped *with Jesus,* crowds gathered *with Jesus,* Pharisees were
afraid to be seen *with Jesus.* The mother of James and John wanted her
two sons to be *with Jesus* in power in heaven. Demons were terrified to
be found *with Jesus,* sinful women and desperate men found sanctuary
with Jesus. Make no mistake; it was all about being *with Jesus!* Because
when you are around a leader long enough, you start to think and act
like that leader.

In the story from Acts 4, we can see that something about Peter has
really changed. Not so long ago, he had denied the Lord three times in
Jesus' most desperate hour. Now we can almost hear Peter say to himself,
"I will not let my Lord down today!" Jesus is the only reason for Peter's
newly found passion. He caught the character of Christ. Jesus' spiritual
strength, courage and resolve rubbed off. There's a definite Christ-

likeness in the Peter who declared God's truth before the Sanhedrin.

This time Peter and John did not run. Standing before the court of Jewish scholars, they felt no shame in being common fishermen from Galilee. They were bold. And confident—so much so that the council of leaders commented about it. The council members must have been

> **If our goal is to teach the truth to our children,**
> **it's likely to be our "modeling," and not our "mouthing,"**
> **that gets the job done.**

thinking: "We are the scholars. We are the ones who went to temple and studied with the Rabbi. Yet they've quoted the Scriptures and it is a more reasonable interpretation than we have ever given. Why are they not afraid to speak about the things of God in our presence? Where did they get their power? Their confidence?"

The short answer: "God chose the foolish things of the world to shame the wise; God chose the weak things of the world to shame the strong" (1 Corinthians 1:27).

What was their conclusion? "They realized they had been with Jesus."

This is the greatest compliment that could ever be paid. If our goal is to teach the truth to our children, the truths about God's design for love, intimacy and sexual health, it's likely to be our "modeling," not our "mouthing," that gets the job done. Jesus understood this from the beginning; mentoring isn't a program or a curriculum. Mentoring is spelled W.I.T.H!

Early in our ministry, my family moved from Oregon to northern New Jersey, just 30 miles from New York City. It was a missionary move as

real as moving overseas. This was a culture shock! People in Jersey ate different things, spoke faster and interrupted more, laughed more quietly, dressed more formally and drove a car...well...with more intensity.

So what happened? Sorry to say they didn't become like me. I ate ziti, learned to talk fast and interrupt more, laugh more quietly, wear a tie

and drive like a maniac! I took on the character of those I was with. I took on the values of my community. Some said I even had a bit of a New Jersey accent. Nah!

BE PERSON-APPROPRIATE

Most of our parents spoke to us very little about sex, love and relationships. It was a rare mom or dad of the 1950s and 1960s who braved this subject matter with their growing children. Our American culture was still very closed about sexuality.

The culture of sexuality exploded during the latter years of the Vietnam War, and the sexual revolution was born. But this revolution almost seems mild compared to our sexually saturated culture of today.

A child or teen can hardly get out of bed without being bombarded with sexual messages. The message begins the moment the alarm clock comes on with music. There are roadside billboards on the way to school. Hallway chatter deals with subjects we cannot fathom. Recess can become a competition to win boyfriends and girlfriends even in third and fourth grades. Then the television goes on after school with sexual saturation on even the most family-friendly sitcoms. Turning on the computer and going into e-mail is almost always a battleground with pornography coming to our children without any effort on their part to find it. The enemy has brought the war zone into our very homes. We try to shelter our kids from harmful lies about sexuality, but it's a never-ending battle.

For this very reason, human sexuality is one of the most important topics to discuss in our Christian families. Our children must know the truth that God has given us in the Bible, and they must know the truth about sex, love and relationships. Sex is one of the main topics on kids' minds.

What one word describes what your parent(s) discussed with you about sex, love and relationships?

And what one word describes how you felt during that discussion?

We want to teach our kids about God's precious gift of sexuality, but how and when do we start?

You've already started, even though you may not be aware of it. When children are very young they are keen observers. They have been observing you and your sexual characteristics since they were small. Did they ever ask you why Mommy looks different than Daddy? When children are young they are not afraid to ask questions. In fact, on some days it seems as though all they do is ask questions! You have also been teaching loving relationships by how you love your spouse, your family members and neighbors. So your children know a lot about love and relationships and physical differences before they ever venture out into the school world.

But what do we do when kids ask embarrassing questions? Most of us have heard the story of the little four year old who asked his dad about where he came from. The dad is thinking, "I can't believe this question is already here; he's only four." So clears his throat and twitches, then begins a detailed explanation of the anatomy and physiology of the reproductive system. He proceeds with an excellent description of sexual intercourse and the fertilization process. But after he finishes up the best explanation of labor and delivery that any dad has ever given to a four-year-old son, the little boy shyly asks his question again. "Daddy, I don't understand. What hospital did I get borned in?"

One of the best ways to begin to talk about the special nature of being male and female is to do it naturally as a day unfolds. Every child is different in what they are curious about at what age. Some children will be natural talkers almost from the time they are born. They will ask any question that comes to mind and be perfectly comfortable talking with Mom or Dad about the answer. Some children will never ask a question and be visibly uncomfortable when you bring up any personal subject. And so, as in all areas of parenting, we develop strategies that are different with each child. The only people who think that the same formula works with every child are people who do not have children! Don't think of what's "age-appropriate." Instead, be person-centered. Think, "How can I best answer this individual child's question?"

There is a general rule that as children grow, the sophistication of your answers needs to grow. When three year olds ask, "Daddy, why do boys have a penis and girls don't?" a simple explanation, "That's the way God made us" is usually sufficient to make the child smile and run

A great time to talk to kids about sexuality is when they are in the gap—young enough to ask honest and sometimes embarrassing questions, but at the same time mature enough to begin to understand relationships.

away and play. That's all the information the child needs. If a 13-year-old daughter asks the same question, she may be seeking specific information about the reproductive system. She may need to be taught the exact functions of a penis. It's likely that she's heard a lot of information at school and feels that she's the only one who doesn't really know what's going on. That lack of knowledge makes a young teen feel vulnerable and very uncomfortable.

A great time to talk to kids about sexuality is when they are in the gap—young enough to ask honest and sometimes embarrassing questions, but at the same time mature enough to begin to understand relationships. Fifth grade is the gap year for many kids. Fifth graders are awesome to work with and usually awesome to parent. This is the age for parents to take advantage of this new maturity, because in one to two years these open, honest children will be middle-schoolers. And that usually means they will not feel as open to ask the difficult questions of their parents, but will seek information elsewhere instead. So parents—take action now! In fifth grade, sex is a frequent topic of conversation. This is the time when most kids need to know the true meaning of the word "sex."

One word of caution; be aware that there are many meanings of the word "sex" in today's preteen and teen culture. When most of today's parents grew up, sex meant vaginal sexual intercourse. Sex has many meanings today to children of different ages. It is not unusual to have very young children use the term "sex" for holding hands. Older children and teenagers often believe that oral sex is not "sex," but use slang words such as "blow jobs" to describe this activity. They often talk openly about mutual masturbation calling it "hand jobs." Some teens see anal sex as a way to have sex without the fear of becoming pregnant. When you and your teen or pre-teen talk about sex, make sure you're speaking and understanding the same language.

Teens and pre-teens today need to know the physical and emotional aspects of sexual intercourse. But they also need to understand that to honor God with their bodies means more than just avoiding vaginal intercourse. It means embracing purity across the whole gamut of sexual behaviors.

To equip you to speak about sexuality with your kids, we've included a practical guide at the end of this chapter. It suggests topics you might cover with kids of various ages, along with diagrams and a basic explanation of the reproductive systems.

How well have you done so far in giving your children information about sexuality?

What should be your next step with each child?

WHAT ABOUT TEENAGERS?

Only a parent can determine how much information to give to a child and at what age. It is important, however, to be realistic about how much your kids have been exposed to sexual messages. For parents of teens, we recommend a field trip! All parents should visit their teen's high school early in their freshman year and stay for at least two passing periods. This experience will open your eyes to just how far from your own high school years this generation is regarding sexual behavior. And you may ask, "How is this relevant? After all, this is a public environment, so how is this going to tell me anything about private sexual behavior?" Unless you're visiting a private Christian high school, what you see on your field trip will shock you. Behavior that was relegated to private places and serious relationships when we were teens is now casual and out in the open. And the behaviors are both heterosexual and homosexual in nature.

When parents witness these behaviors on their high school field trip, they assume that kids aren't listening to their parents anymore. Even the federal government thought that was true! Then they started to receive the results from the most thorough and expensive study of high school students ever attempted in the U.S. The ADD Health Study was released in 1997. It shows that *the most important reason teens do not have sex is because their parents do not approve.* Teens are listening! So talk with your teens about your values and morals on the subject of sex outside of marriage. They listen and they act accordingly!

You'll find it much easier to talk with teenagers about sex if you wait for teachable moments rather than sitting down to have "the big talk." Remember, these young people are emerging adults. They need to be treated with respect. Watching a television program or movie together will create opportunities to point out lies and truth. High speed conversations—traveling 65 MPH down the highway—assure that your preteen will stay (literally) with the conversation. And talking in sound bytes rather than long lectures will help both you and your teen feel more comfortable. Make sure your young adult knows that you're available to talk any time.

Do you think your teenager knows all about the anatomy and physiology of the reproductive system? Sure, there's fifth grade puberty class, and abundant talk and speculation in the halls. But even if you've covered this ground yourself, it's a good idea to do a check to see how much has sunk in. Many kids in high school and college lack a basic understanding of the anatomy and physiology of the male and female reproductive systems. Getting those facts straight is a great place to start. Here are a few other topics you might cover during a series of conversations that may last months or years.

- The appropriate age for dating
- What to do on a date
- Curfew
- Drinking and dating
- Sexually transmitted diseases and AIDS
- Family values about:
  - Abortion
  - Sex outside of marriage
  - Contraception
  - Homosexuality
  - Masturbation
  - Pornography
  - Alcohol and drugs

In later chapters, you'll find detailed help in deciding how you want to approach these subjects with your teenager.

How would you describe a teachable moment?

When do teachable moments occur with your child?

What topics do you think are most on your teenager's mind?

One common complaint from teens is judgment from their parents. They often say that when they ask their parents a question about sex, parents automatically assume that they are sexually active. Some teens even say that their parents immediately accuse them of having sex and begin to watch everything they do. Or their parents begin to put unrealistic restrictions on their social life. These barriers to communication are very dangerous. Avoid them! Discipline yourself to listen without jumping to conclusions or overreacting. Do whatever you can to encourage open communication. Honest discussions allow you to guide your teenager in God's truth. Accept the fact that these discussions will involve some discomfort. That's normal and to be expected.

WHAT IF MY TEEN IS HAVING SEX?

If you learn that your teen has had sex or is engaging in unsatisfactory behavior according to your family values, talk to your teen with your spouse present. Make this a private conversation with only you as

Remember, these young people are emerging adults.

They need to be treated with respect.

parents and your teenager. Never confront your teen in front of siblings or guests in your home. Treat your teen with dignity and love, but confront directly. Ask direct questions. "Are you having sex?" "How long have you been having sex?" If your daughter is having sex, ask if she has had a pregnancy test. If your son is having sex, ask if his girlfriend has had a pregnancy test. Ask if they have been checked for STDs. Then take whatever action you and your spouse believe is appropriate for your family.

Believe it or not, many teens are relieved when their parents discover their sexual activity. Many teens do not want to be sexually active and are coerced or manipulated into such behavior. You may have an initially angry teen on your hands but, in time, he or she will experience great relief to be out of the cycle of guilt, shame and lying.

Yes, you can talk about sex with your kids! And they will listen. Decide to do it.

WHAT DO THEY NEED TO KNOW WHEN?

Preschoolers

- Answer only the question the child asks.
- Give a short, simple explanation in words that are common in your child's vocabulary.
- Explain any difficult words.
- Don't ignore questions; this will cause confusion about sex and can imply that sex is bad.
- Always keep in the back of your mind that you want to communicate through the years that sex is awesome in the context of marriage.

Ages 5–8

- We grow up in many ways including physically, mentally, emotionally and spiritually.
- God made you and you're the only you! You are awesome in all ways.
- We can control all of our behaviors. We need to practice self-control every day.
- We all deserve respect.
- Boys and girls are different in many ways.

  - A girl's body develops in ways that allow a woman to become pregnant and give birth to children.

  - A boy's body develops in ways that allow a man to be a father.

  - All of our body parts are special and are created by God. We need to show our body respect and take care of it every day.

Ages 9–12

- As we enter puberty, our bodies change. We all change at different times. God planned it that way. See pages 25–27 for diagrams and explanations you might find helpful in talking with your child.
- As our bodies change, we feel new urges. These are sexual urges.
- Sex is a wonderful gift from God for married people. It brings a husband and wife closer in their relationship. This is called intimacy, and it is good.
- God wants us to wait until we are married to have sex. We are capable of self-control. We use it every day in other areas of our lives.
- God wants us to be careful what we allow ourselves to see and hear and do.
- The Bible tells us how God wants us to use the gift of sexuality.

- God created us in a way that we can think through right and wrong behavior, including choices we make about sex.

Ages 12–15

- Review the physiology and anatomy of sex.
- All of us have sexual feelings. But feelings are different than behaviors. We can control our behavior with the choices we make.
- All sex is sex. God calls us to save sex for marriage.
- Marriage between a man and a woman provides a stable relationship that helps children to grow into healthy adults.
- God calls us to follow his rules within the Bible to protect us physically, emotionally, mentally and spiritually.
- Having sexual partners outside of marriage has physical and psychological consequences that may never go away.

Ages 16–18

- The joy of marrying a person who has waited to give you the gift of his or her sexuality is one of God's greatest gifts to you.
- Sex is never an obligation.
- Sex is not love. Love is not sex.
- Love is unconditional and is never earned.
- Trust is always earned and is not unconditional
- Being sexually pure (no sexual activity) before marriage decreases the chance of damage to the reproductive system from STDs.
- Condoms do little to protect against the most common STDs.
- AIDS is destroying entire cultures in some parts of the world.
- Sexual abuse is widespread in our society. If you know or suspect you have been sexually abused immediately seek help from a parent, pastor, priest or counselor.

"THE TALK"

Most children ask questions well before any parent would think of sitting down and talking to them about the changes in puberty and how babies are created. And talking with our children usually begins with their questions and continues on different levels throughout their lifetime. It is not just one talk. But if your child is in the fifth grade and has not begun to ask questions about puberty, this is a good time to have a beginning talk.

But what do you say? How do you begin? Having a pamphlet or booklet to talk with and show pictures is always a good idea. This allows something to be left behind for your child to read in privacy and to refer back to as a guide. But make sure that you and your spouse are in complete agreement as to the contents of the booklet. Sometimes booklets have some very good information but also include information that may be inconsistent with your family values.

Choose a private setting for this talk. It's not appropriate to include siblings and friends in this very private time. If at all possible have the same-sex parent deliver the talk. This will be much more comfortable for the child. And the setting should be relaxed and comfortable to help the subject matter be more comfortable for you and your child.

What follows here is a sample script. This is by no means meant to substitute your words or language. It is simply a guide to understand what typical fifth graders need to know and what they typically understand regarding puberty and human reproduction. Share the diagrams with your child at a level you are both comfortable with. Continue into the subject of sex and fertilization to the comfort level of you and your child.

Sometime between the ages of 10 and 18 in girls and between the ages of 12 and 16 for boys, changes begin to happen very quickly. These changes cause a girl to change into a woman and a boy to change into a man. This time is called *puberty* or *adolescence*. It's a time full of physical changes (changes of the body), emotional changes (feelings), mental changes (thoughts) and spiritual changes (thoughts about God). And while it can be exciting to see and experience these changes, they can be disturbing, too. There are a lot of changes to get used to!

The changes on the inside and the outside of the body have to do with changes in the brain. Deep down inside of the brain is a very powerful gland called the *pituitary gland*. This gland is small—about the size of a pea—but it's very powerful. One day the pituitary gland starts to release *hormones* that travel to your *reproductive system*. Hormones are really little chemical messengers that tell your body to do something. In this case the hormones tell your reproductive system to begin to change and grow into adulthood. And the reproductive system is the system of the body that allows humans to reproduce themselves or have babies.

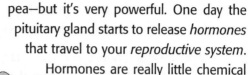

Hormones

Chemical Messengers

For a girl the hormones from the pituitary gland tell her *ovaries* in her reproductive system to start to make a large amount of another hormone called *estrogen*. The increase in estrogen causes a girl's body to take on the characteristics of an adult woman's body. These changes include the enlargement of breasts (to be able to feed a baby one day), the narrowing of the waist and the broadening of the hips (to allow a baby to pass through one day during the birth process). These hormones also cause her voice to become softer and for hair to start to grow under the arms and in the *pubic area*.

Another change that occurs for girls is that she will begin her *menstrual cycle* and begin to menstruate or have her *periods*. Remember the word ovaries? Females have two ovaries in the reproductive system. These ovaries have all of the *eggs* or *ovum* that she will ever need to have children some day. In fact there are over 300,000 eggs in female ovaries. After puberty begins one egg will ripen and be released from one of the

Ovary
Fallopian Tube
Uterus
Bladder
Rectum
Urethra
Vagina
Anus

ovaries each month. This happens about once per month from about the age of 10–16 until the age of 50–60. After the egg or ovum is released from one of the ovaries it travels down a *fallopian tube* into the *uterus*. The uterus is also called the *womb* in the Bible. The uterus is where one day a baby may grow for about nine months before he or she is born.

At the time the egg is released the uterus is building up a lining. If the egg is not *fertilized* (a baby is not created) the lining of the uterus is shed. This lining comes to the outside of the body for several days, and this is called menstruation.

Day 1 to 5   **Day 6 to 13**   **Day 14 to 16**   **Day 17 to 28**

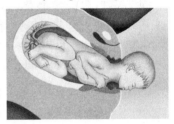

If the egg is fertilized and a baby begins to grow, the uterus is the perfect place for the baby to develop for nine months. Then it will be ready to come out through the woman's vagina.

For a boy the hormones from the pituitary gland tell his *testes* to begin to make and release a large amount of a hormone called *testosterone*. Testosterone causes the male body to change from a boy into a man. Shoulders begin to broaden and the waist and hips narrow. The voice deepens gradually and facial hair begins to appear (very slowly for most boys). Hair also begins to thicken on the legs and arms and hair on the chest begins to appear slowly. Hair begins to grow under the arms and in the *pubic area*. The reproductive body parts, including the *penis* and *scrotum*, become larger and begin to produce semen and sperm.

Soon after changes appear on the outside of the body the penis begins to spontaneously become erect or hard. This is something that can happen

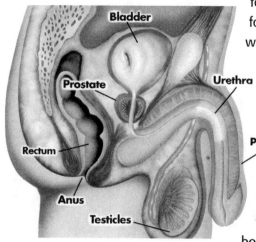

for no reason at all. It only lasts for a short time and no one will notice. But it can be embarrassing the first few times it happens. Also the reproductive system can become full of sperm (the male reproductive cell) and semen (the fluid that sperm live in) and need to empty some of the fluid to the outside of the body. This often happens in the middle of the night and is called a *nocturnal emission* or *wet dream*. This is also perfectly normal, but it is a change that one needs to get used to.

And so for both boys and girls there are many new changes. But the terrific thing about all of the changes is that we know they are all a part of God's plan for us. He created our bodies to work just the way they work. And soon the changes will be finished and you will be the awesome man or woman that he created you to be!

THE BATTLE
at your
Doorstep

Think of it this way.

You are the king. A mounting army of evil warriors has pitched their tents just outside the boundaries of your land. You know these warriors. They are the same ones who destroyed a kingdom just to the north. They killed the male children 14 and younger. They raped and tortured the girls and women to get the men to surrender. They put hooks through the mouths of the men worthy of work and marched them 400 miles back to their land. The old and injured men they killed, slowly.

They have been forming their forces to overtake you. They will soon shut off the water supply and the trade roads that lead to your land. All that you hold dear is at risk. Your family, land, heritage and security stand in the shadow of this looming disaster.

Now here's the surprising part. If you act first, you know that the enemy will run. These warriors who have come to attack have no real courage. Their motivation to fight comes from their evil lord who kills deserters and the weak soldiers in his own army to maintain the allegiance of his troops. These warriors live in fear of their own evil king. Their best fighters are mercenaries who fight for anyone who pays them. Loyalty is shallow. At the first sign of battle, the best warriors flee.

As king, you know you have the forces to defeat this army. Your kingdom is the richest in the world. You have plenty of well trained fighters and a real reason to fight. Your men have the best weapons; they lack for no resources.

You have seen it before. Kingdoms just like yours have fallen to a lesser foe. Not because you *can't* win, but because you *won't* win. The very thing that makes you strong has numbed your army into sleepiness. You are rich and comfortable. The enemy has been

We are in a battle for our children and teenagers
and we must take every care to be ready and armed.

approaching for years, but they have never done anything to you directly—so far. Oh, they have killed some who lived just outside your kingdom. But they have never directly attacked the kingdom. They have been careful to rob and kill only those who cannot fight back. Your kingdom has virtually forgotten the evil army is there.

But that's changing. Incredibly, you have found out recently that members of your own army have been doing business with these killers, and making an incredible profit. You are out of time. You must move quickly. You have become aware that the enemy intends to strike while the kingdom sleeps. In only hours all may be lost. If your armies will just hear your voice and follow your orders, your kingdom will be saved. If they hear, obey and come to arms, the outcome is assured.

You are king. What will you do? What will you say? What will the army do?

This word picture is directly from God. It is right from Scripture. Late in his life, Paul is imprisoned awaiting his execution. He has served his Lord and King, Jesus, for many years at great personal cost. He is aware that a cosmic struggle is taking place between the forces of good and evil, and while the final outcome of the battle is not in question, the collateral damage from this war cannot be measured in terms of human suffering. He knows that the only thing standing between these forces and our destruction is obedience to King Jesus. The king Paul serves is Master of all Creation; no foe can stand before him. And God has given us authority to use this power to vanquish the foes of God. Paul wrote of it to his friends at Ephesus and Corinth, encouraging them and calling them to arms:

> *Finally, be strong in the Lord and in his mighty power. Put on the full armor of God so that you can take your stand against the devil's schemes. For our struggle is not against flesh and blood, but against the rulers, against the authorities, against the powers of this dark world and against the spiritual forces of evil in the heavenly realm* (Ephesians 6:10–12).

> *The weapons we fight with are not the weapons of the world. On the contrary, they have divine power to demolish strongholds* (2 Corinthians 10:4).

Paul's fear is not that the army of God *can't* win against these foes, but that they *won't*. He saw a church beginning to become distracted by things of the world. These distractions included things like money, comfort, power and influence. So he called the church to arms. This is what he said to his most trusted field general, Timothy, when he saw the foe braced to attack.

> *Endure hardship with us like a good soldier of Christ Jesus. No one serving as a soldier gets involved in civilian affairs—he wants to please his commanding officer. Similarly, if anyone competes as an athlete, he does not receive the victor's crown unless he competes according to the rules. The hardworking farmer should be the first to receive a share of the crops. Reflect on what I am saying, for the Lord will give you insight into all this* (2 Timothy 2:3–8).

Will you stand and fight for all you hold dear and true? We are in a battle for our children and teenagers and we must take every care to be ready and armed, for the evil one is biding his time. The evil one is telling them lies and tempting them to ruin. God has called us to war. Will you fight to save your children and family? The battle is at your doorstep!

What weapons does Satan use against you to keep you from talking to your kids?

What other analogy would help you prepare spiritually to talk to your kids about sexuality?

BATTLE SHY

Perhaps in the course of your life you've made some sexual choices you're not proud of. Can you really talk to your kids about making Christ-honoring choices when you failed to do so yourself? Now hear this: that's one of Satan's lies! He wants to make you feel that you're unworthy to parent, too sinful to confront and too soiled to challenge someone else to be clean.

In your head the battle might sound something like this: "It's wrong for me to say anything to my children. God can never use a sinner like me. I am so messed up that I wonder if I am really a Christian. My heart is wicked, and I am a loser who doesn't deserve the promises of God."

Many of us grew up in the 60s and 70s, and we made a lot of mistakes with our own sexuality. Some participated in sex, had abortions and experimented with drugs. We feel tainted by these choices and fearful of tackling subjects that might make us vulnerable. Is it realistic to expect our kids to achieve a higher standard than we did?

There's a nagging fear that when we bring up the subject of sex, our kids will ask questions about our experiences. How will kids feel about us if they know about the past? They might conclude, "Well, you turned out all right. It can't be so bad."

Don't listen to the evil one. He is the voice of deception and there is no truth in him.

Here's the good news. If you are a Christian, God has given you a new heart, a heart devoted to his own purposes. You are his beloved, the son or daughter of the king, entitled to every power and blessing and responsibility that goes with the position of a prince or princess!

Listen to this:

It is no longer I myself who do it, but it is sin living in me. I know that nothing good lives in me; that is, my sinful nature....Now if I do what I do not want to do, it is no longer I who do it, but it is the sin living in me that does it....For in my inner being, in my heart of hearts, I delight in God's law!" (Romans 7:17, 18, 20, 22)

When you came to Christ, you became a new creature. All of your sins have been forgiven. Your heart attitude is not to sin, but this verse reminds us that when we do sin, it is an old habit that dies hard. You, the real you, is remade. You hate sin. You are not disqualified from talking to your kids about sex. Your slate is clean. Your forgiven state is no different than any other great saint in history.

A. W. Tozer wrote:

It becomes the devil's business to keep the Christian's spirit imprisoned. He knows that the believing and justified Christian has been raised up out of the grave of his sins and trespasses.

From that point on, Satan works that much harder to keep us bound and gagged, actually imprisoned in our own grave clothes. He knows that if we continue in this kind of bondage...we are not much better off than when we were spiritually dead.

What are some of the circumstances in your life that have made you feel disqualified to share the truth?

THE BATTLE AT YOUR DOORSTEP | 33

What would it take for you to feel qualified again?

IT'S NOT TOO LATE

Many parents feel that eight and nine year olds are too young for conversations about sex. The truth is, this is a perfect time to talk about general issues of right and wrong. Some topics that may lay groundwork for later sexual decisions include how to treat friends and how to be honoring to adults.

If we missed that chance to talk about right and wrong, we think, "Well, I can still talk to them about the hard core biology of sex in sixth grade." But then the school gets there first and we just kind of let it go, secretly glad that the dirty work is done.

So we set our sights on helping them understand love in high school. But by the time that happens they don't seem to want to hear our opinions anymore.

Satan begins to whisper again. "You missed your chance. They don't listen to you anymore. You aren't important. As a parent you have failed and you might as well get used to the idea that your child trusts friends more than you." Sound familiar? Those are age-old lies of Satan. He is a practiced, skillful liar.

Don't give in. Instead, learn some new skills. Attack an old problem in a creative way.

A few years ago I had a family coming into counseling. The "problem" they came in to "fix" was their daughter. Anna was 14. According to her parents she wasn't listening to her mom and dad anymore. She was growing distant and rebellious.

DAVE'S STORY

When I talked to Anna, she was hesitant. Professionals had ganged up on her before, and she didn't want to go through that again. As I spent time with her, I discovered that Anna was a very nice young lady who wasn't trying to be mean and rebel—she was simply trying to figure out things for herself. Her parents didn't like the way

she was experimenting with clothes and hanging out with new friends. They felt unloved and she felt alone and distrusted.

I'd heard of a family who worked through difficult issues by writing messages on pieces of paper, folding them into airplanes and flying them into the room of the person they were angry with. I encouraged Anna's family to try this method of communication. Taking time to write out their thoughts slowed things down and kept them from getting too wrapped up in the emotions of the moment. Conversations became more thoughtful and productive.

Anna's family thought they'd lost the opportunity to speak with their daughter. They were delighted to discover that their ability to talk things over with Anna hadn't passed them by—it just needed to take a different form.

Don't give up on talking with your young adult, no matter how daunting the task may seem. Explore creative ways to communicate and keep those lines open!

DO YOU LIKE WHAT THEY SEE?

Satan tries to confuse and confound us with messages like, "I am just so tired and numb. I wonder if anything I do matters in their lives. I go to games, they don't care. I help with homework, they don't turn it in. I fix their car or help them get to work when they miss the bus and I get no thanks. I am getting tired of it all. It doesn't matter if I show up or don't show up. Nothing I do counts as love."

This is another terrible lie. Don't you believe it!

Pay special attention to these next two concepts. They'll make a tremendous difference in your motivation as a parent and help you deflect Satan's lie that what you invest in parenting is ineffective.

1. Your smallest sin is more devastating to the cause of Christ than you can imagine. Every act of disobedience sets into motion a cycle of sadness, with ripple effects that transcend our understanding. When one in the Body of Christ sins, the rest of us in the Body suffer.

When you sin against your children, Satan will attack you with lies and your pride will swell. You will not want to go to them and confess and say you are sorry. But you must. You will want them to take the first steps toward reconciliation. But you're the mature adult, older and wiser. You have the ability to model humility and gentleness and self-control. This is your chance to model integrity at home, the most important place in the world.

You are modeling all the time. It's just that sometimes you are modeling pride and anger and bitterness. Sometimes we just want to win because we can. We feel like we've earned the right to win. If we don't get our way, we're tempted to punish without thinking instead of disciplining in a Spirit-led manner.

As parents we understand that this is a long distance run, not a sprint. This is about 25 years, not 25 minutes.

This is a sobering piece of information. The good news follows.

2. The smallest act of obedience has more merit than you can imagine. Jesus says even the simple act of offering a cup of cold water in his name will not go unnoticed. Jesus has a habit of taking our most modest offerings to him and multiplying them.

   This is true when we make sacrifices for our kids. They may not notice your sacrifice. In fact they may think they are entitled to your sacrifice. But you are still modeling. You are modeling attitude and motive and a giving spirit. As parents we understand that this is a long distance run, not a sprint. This is about 25 years, not 25 minutes. Our eyes have to be on the modeling for a lifetime, not for today.

   What you do, what you say, the time you invest—all of this matters more than you can ever believe. Parenting just might be the ultimate example of delayed gratification. We'd like to see results *now.* We could go a long time on just a small word of gratitude that never seems to come. Realize that there's more than human effort involved here. God is taking your efforts and multiplying them. Keep trying and trusting God to bless your efforts. The smallest investment you make in your young adult's life may bear fruit you never see.

> **How hard is it for you to admit to your kids that you've wronged them? Why do you think that is?**

> **What positive things do your kids see in you, even if they never acknowledge it?**

SAY YES FROM YOUR KNEES

J. R. R. Tolkein's *The Lord of the Rings* is a rich, visual allegory. The series of movies has brought the message to a wide audience that readily identifies with the struggle of each character. The world of evil is so evil and the struggle seems so real. The story line reminds us of the Scripture passage we talked about earlier. Frodo and his companions find themselves in a battle of cosmic proportions. It's not just about swords and strategy. It's a spiritual battle to hang on to goodness in the face of overwhelming evil.

In these fantasies, the world of Middle Earth is at war. Frodo, a hobbit, is sent on a desperate trip through the evil land of Mordor to destroy the Ring of Sauron, the most powerful and evil wizard on earth. To help him in this brave task, a fellowship forms. Representatives of all the good creatures of Middle Earth stand together in a nearly hopeless battle against overwhelming evil. Together they form the Fellowship of the Ring.

Today we as Christians are at war, against powers and principalities that we cannot see. The enemy is more ugly and destructive than a band of orcs, and the consequences are staggering and eternal. The field of battle doesn't lie in an imaginary land. It's in our homes, schools, neighborhoods and malls. Within our families we need to form a fellowship that supports our kids in the fight against sexual sin. "Love" gone wrong is the weapon on destruction. The battle is daily, and our defense is God's truth.

Remember Paul's words to Timothy? Do you hear them as though they are spoken to us today?

"Will you suffer hardship with me as a good soldier? Will you commit to fight with me and not entangle yourself with the affairs of everyday life, so that together we may please the one who enlisted us as soldiers?"

Remember in Isaiah 6, where Isaiah saw the Lord seated on his throne high and exalted? The sight caused Isaiah to fall on his face in fear, knowing that he was a man of unclean lips and that he lived among a people of unclean lips. The Lord sent angels, cherubim, each with six wings, to take a coal from the ever burning altar. With that coal they touched his lips and made them clean. Then as the Lord asked, "Who will go for Me, who shall I send?" Isaiah responded in his new condition of understanding, forgiveness and readiness, "Here am I. Send me!"

The grace of God heals you from the wounds of the past so that you can look to the future of your children.

God has given you a Counselor to help in the tough situations when you don't know what to say.

Because Jesus Christ died for you, you can walk in the Spirit and model what you want your kids to see.

Unload the baggage that holds you back from what you want to do. Turn away from Satan's lies and embrace the power of God's truth. Join the Fellowship of the King. This Fellowship will devote itself to prayer for this generation of youth, and we will stand fast against the wiles of the devil. Because our kids are worth it!

chapter three

KIds
In
Context

Anyone who has watched Music Television (MTV) is aware that they play it close to the edge. Really close to the edge. This music and entertainment showcase specializes in a 13–40 year-old predominantly male audience. At various hours you can find sexually explicit images matched with heart pounding rhythms of rap and hip-hop, and just a few hours later you might watch a show dedicated to sexual health. Over its history, MTV has censored itself and the music videos they broadcast. But their standards, just like everyone else's, have loosened in recent years.

A 2000 study by the Parents Television Council (PTC) showed that what most of us think really is true: the amount of sex and violence on prime-time television has gotten worse. In addition to reporting the number of incidents of offensive occurrences, the study shows the increasingly graphic nature of sexual images over a 10-year span. The number of sexual references per hour during prime-time television tripled during the 1990s, but looking at what the references are is even more revealing. References to sexual subjects grew across the board: kinky sex (357%), genitals (650%) and masturbation (700%). The increase in references to homosexuality during prime-time TV topped all subjects at 2,650%.[1]

TV isn't the only thing that has changed since we were kids. Teens today were born between the mid-1980s and 1990. By the time they were able to read many of them had computers in their homes. This gave them access to really good things like interactive learning programs and fun games to play with "real" foes. But it has given them something that no other generation before them has confronted: instant access to pornography. Many parents remember the days when it was scandalous to show beds—even twin beds—in a married couple's bedroom on TV. In those days, parents would rip the pages of lingerie ads from the Sears and Roebuck catalog so that their children wouldn't see sexual body parts or partial nudity. Now after we teach our puberty program to fifth graders and their parents, we almost always have parents come to us and ask what they can do with their fifth grade son because they fear that he's already addicted to pornography. There is no comparison between the sexual images that our children see today and what most of us were exposed to in childhood.

**Over the last 20 years, what kind of changes
have you noticed in what TV will show on the air?**

What shows do you now find the most offensive and why?

**How have your personal viewing habits changed
in the past five years?**

U.S. YOUTH CULTURE AND SEXUAL ACTIVITY

Young people are a bit of a mystery. Because there are so many and because they are so diverse, it's difficult to get a good beat on their behaviors, especially their sexual behaviors. One thing about this generation is that these young people are willing to talk! They may have lots of misinformation, but they are not shy!

The Henry H. Kaiser Family Foundation surveyed 1,800 scientifically selected individuals age 13 to 24, compiled the research and reported it in 2003. The survey asked frank questions about all kinds of high-risk behavior. Because it is associated with a health care agency, the Kaiser Foundation was particularly interested in looking at adolescent sexual behavior. They know that the earlier a person begins sexual activity and the more sexual partners a person has, the more the person is at risk when it comes to adolescent pregnancy and sexually transmitted diseases. This study comes from a more liberal perspective than some, but the study and research work is well designed. Their data is extremely helpful to look at, as they have been doing these studies long enough to see some trends. Here are some of the findings:[2]

Respondents Concerns
- Young people are more concerned about sex* and sexual health than any other health issues in their lives.
- Four out of five teens and young adults say they are personally concerned about how sexual health may affect them.
- This survey found that even among 13 and 14 year olds, the majority are strongly concerned about sex and relationships.

Sexual Activity and Behaviors
- Nearly 2/3 of high school seniors have had sex.
- 1/3 of all adolescents have engaged in oral sex.
- 75% of all sexually active adolescents have engaged in oral sex.

Oral Sex and Beliefs
- 25% of sexually active teens report that oral sex is a strategy to avoid sexual intercourse.
- More than two out of five do not consider it to be as big a deal as sexual intercourse.
- 33% of teens stated that oral sex is safer sex.

Unmarried Pregnancy

- Over one million teen pregnancies occur in the U.S. each year.
- 10% of girls between 15–19 become pregnant.
- Seven out of ten sexually active young adults have had a pregnancy test or have had a partner who took a pregnancy test.
- Nearly one in four sexually active young people contract an STD every year.
- 50% of all new HIV infections in the U.S. occur among people under the age of 25.

STD Misinformation

- While 75% of sexually active teens engage in oral sex, 20% of teens are unaware that STDs can be transmitted through this activity.
- 20% of teens stated that they would simply "know " if someone had an STD.
- 20% of young people believe that birth control pills offer protection from STDs and HIV.

Relationships

- For both adolescents and young adults pressure to have sex is exceeded only by pressure to drink. One third of the respondents say they have been in relationships where sexual activity has moved forward faster than they wanted.
- *Keep in mind that the when the word "sex" is written it means vaginal sexual intercourse. Oral and anal sex and mutual masturbation may not be recorded here.*

Teen sexual activity is a difficult subject to examine. It's an emotional subject. Many parents, especially moms, think it's cute to see their little girl or boy in a relationship with the opposite sex. It brings a wave of nostalgia that reflects back to their own sexual awakenings. And for the most part it's exciting to watch as children discover that opposite gender relationships can be satisfying.

But the looming question for most parents today is whether their kids' opposite sex friendships are innocent or whether there is sexual involvement. Is the world a safe place for this exploration? Are our family values being pushed too far? Let's take a look at how our perspectives are changing.

UNDERSTANDING THE MILLENNIALIST TIMELINE

Perhaps a good way to understand today's youth culture is to try to see life from their viewpoint. We can see what kinds of things this generation has never been without, and how that might affect their perspective on life.

Teens today have never lived without instant food. The microwave oven was first distributed in the early 1980s. They have always had instant access to information with pictures through the television. They have always had instant access to international information through cable television. They have instant access to communication on cell phones and instant messenger services on their computers.

They have more things designed to entertain them—video games, magazines, music and movies, all designed especially for them. This dynamic of being entertained has become a consuming reality for this culture. The ultimate sin is to be bored.

Their concept of reality is blurred. They have always lived with special effects, death that does not kill, violence that does not hurt and casual sex that does not have any consequences.

Our children have grown up—the first entire generation to do so— in a culture where divorce seems almost the norm. The divorce rate hit 50% in 1976 and has remained high since then, coming back down a very few ticks every year since. The cultural impression for many if not most teens is that they will be in a broken home at some time in their lives. Being in a culture where to be with your nuclear family unit is unusual has huge emotional and psychological consequences. Many children are left with the feeling that at any time their family life as they know it may be ripped apart. Many are living with a constant unconscious fear of family insecurity, even when their family is healthy and not at risk of divorce.

Oddly, some teens see privilege and opportunity in families being separated. Their sense of reality is so skewed that they can become jealous of the gifts and competition for attention some children of divorce experience. One teen with a sad look on her face said that she wished her parents were divorced so she could have time off from her mom and dad when she would switch houses.

Today's teens live in a world of sexually explicit images and influences that are not just *available* but *predatory* in nature. Prior to about 1980, in order to watch a movie, a person had to go to a theater or rent the actual film. Video Cassette Recorders (VCRs) were not yet on the scene. To find pornographic magazines a teen had to get access to an adult who had pornography around. Even adults had to sneak off to an "adult" bookstore or theater and hope that no one they knew saw them entering or leaving.

All that has changed. Teens today have lived with instant access to pornography all their lives. It can be rented and watched anonymously at someone's home. Many teens have friends whose parents have sophisticated collections of pornography that teenagers have access to. Many cable TV services offer soft-core pornographic movies on a regular basis, and some cable stations exist only to offer pornography 24 hours a day, seven days a week. Hotels offer X-rated movies with the added benefit of keeping the specific movie private. Major bookstore chains offer sections on "Erotica," a euphemism for porn.

The Internet offers instant access to sexual images and sexual depravity that only 15 years ago would have been impossible for most normal adult populations to even imagine, much less find. It is very different from the time we grew up.

How does it make you feel when you think of your kids being exposed to explicit sexual images at a young age?

What do you think are the cultural consequences for our youth because of their access to pornography for their entire lifetime?

Another reality that is dramatically different from what we as parents experienced growing up is the prevalence of sexually transmitted disease (STDs). When the "Sexual Revolution" of the 1960s took place, the boundary of decency and morality was broken with relatively few consequences. There were only two diseases that Baby Boomers had to watch out for, gonorrhea and syphilis. Both are bacterial infections and easily cured. At the time those who participated did not know they were laying the groundwork for a generation of psychological disorders.

Many of today's youth get sex education starting in grade five (some at grade three or even kindergarten) and it begins with conversations on disease and condom use. The innocence of sex has been ushered out and replaced by unrealistic fantasy played by our

> **They have always lived with special effects,**
> **death that does not kill, violence that does not hurt and**
> **casual sex that does not have any consequences.**

favorite "Friends" on TV. Few TV characters ever get pregnant or infected, but our teens know that dozens of their friends have HPV, herpes or chlamydia. One image endorses the idea that they are "immortal" and should be free to try everything. The reality in their school and neighborhood is that they may never be able to rid themselves of a disease, have a baby or find a life partner they can trust.

Teens today live in a world of terrorism that has struck them at home. Never before have we experienced real actions of war against Americans on American soil. Teens now know they live in a dangerous world. And they know the world is full of lies. They now realize that their fantasy of living in a safe world will never be reality. Psychologists and sociologists cannot predict how this will affect our youth. We can expect that sociological research studies on traumatized youth from nations like Israel and Lebanon soon will show up in the U.S. journals of mental health. We want to help care for them and protect them, but some threats are lodged at the very heart of their culture.

**Do you feel hopeful or scared when you take a hard
look at the circumstances our youth find themselves in?**

**Where do feel or see the most distress?
Where do you have the most hope?**

DISTURBING TRENDS AND TRUE LIFE HOPE

One of the most disturbing trends we have observed regarding teen sexual activity in Christians is the thought that sex is only defined as vaginal sexual intercourse. Teens seem to be saying that God is only concerned whether they are "technical virgins" when they are married. This is illustrated in George Barna's research of 2001. He found that 83% of Christian teens believe that moral truth depends on the circumstances, and only 6% believe that moral truth is absolute.[3]

These ideas of technical virginity and truth not being absolute are reflected in the increasing practice of oral sex. The study by The Henry H. Kaiser Family Foundation of 2003 reported, "25% of sexually active teens report that oral sex is a strategy to avoid sexual intercourse and that more than two out of five do not consider it to be as big of a deal as sexual intercourse."[4]

A mom called me very irate and needing to talk. She said that at her son's middle school they just found two couples during lunch performing oral sex. One couple was in the alley behind the school and one couple was beneath one of the lunch tables. These children were in seventh grade.

LINDA'S STORY

Over and over again in the past five years we have found that churched youth do not consider behaviors other than vaginal intercourse to be sex. Rachel, a high school sophomore, said that there are lots of ways to keep her boyfriend happy other than intercourse. There was a low rumble of laughter in the youth room as other youth shook their heads and smiled. Oral sex, anal sex, mutual masturbation and sleepovers with the opposite sex are seen as acceptable in many youth groups. So where does this leave our youth culture? And where does this leave us as a Christian youth culture?

How can teens distinguish between right and wrong when they are trying to make sexual decisions on the run and everything the world offers seems right and truthful?

Here is what we know. Teens are, as a group, insecure. They have unconscious fears of abandonment and live with a sense of dread, not hope. This is the first generation that when surveyed reported that they do not believe that their generation will be better off than their parents. We do know that older elementary kids, preteens and teenagers are acting out in this environment by seeking love and security and significance in opposite sex relationships very early. When most parents grew up it was rare to see a boyfriend and girlfriend holding hands until late junior high school or early senior high school. That is not the case today.

All this information leaves us with the profound awareness that we can no longer protect our kids. We can't shelter them. We have to prepare them. And here is the kicker! Education alone does not prepare them!

How can teens distinguish between right and wrong when they are trying to make sexual decisions on the run and everything the world offers seems right and truthful? The answer is to have loving mature relationships in their lives that help them steer through all this danger. It has been said that, *"Speaking the truth without love is cruelty."*

Teens don't need more "in your face truth." They don't need more clichés and "Just say no" campaigns. They need the truth spoken to them in the context of a loving relationship. Trisha can tell it best.

TRISHA'S STORY

I came to Christ when I was six years old. My family and I had always gone to church. One night my mom was praying with me before I fell asleep and I asked her if I could give my life to Christ right then. I remember it all very clearly. Church was very important to my family and though my church was very small and conservative, I really liked it. I loved my friends there and my Sunday school classes.

When I was 13 we had a presentation in my middle school class about sexual purity and I signed a pledge card committing to save myself sexually and to remain pure for my future husband. My parents bought me a pledge ring and I still have it. I began wearing it every day.

In my first year of high school I fell in love with Steve. He was the first boy I dated, and though we really didn't go out on dates, he was allowed to come over to my house to have dinner with my parents or to go with us to church.

And then it happened. The first time we kissed it was as though something went off inside of me. Even though I was only 14 years old I began to believe that I had found my future husband and that God had answered that prayer for me. We found even more moments to be alone and the kissing began to get more intense and eventually, quickly, we started with even more intimate behavior.

Then one evening we were doing homework together at his house and we were all alone. Steve and I had sex.

Again it was as though something went off in me. I had broken my pledge. We both made promises that this would never happen again. But it did. Three more times. And each time I felt more shame and guilt and more confused.

The last time I had sex, my period was late and I thought that I was pregnant. I was so scared. I couldn't imagine how this perfect Christian girl from this perfect Christian family was going to live this down. I was so afraid.

About that time my mom came home and found me sitting alone in the living room. She just kind of walked up to me and said, "Trisha, have you slept with Steve?" I wanted to lie, I tried to lie. I had been able to lie about our behavior before, but this time I just broke down and started to cry. I thought my mom would kill me. She was a little angry, but she was more sad. She kept saying "We will get through this," and then the really scary thing: "We have to tell your dad.'"

That night I had to go through the whole thing again. It was the first time I had ever seen my dad cry. I was so sorry for disappointing him. I thought that they would kill me, but they were great. I found out soon I was not pregnant and that was really good news. I was too young to have a child. My parents grounded me and took away a lot of privileges but I was okay with that. They even had Steve over and had a time of prayer with him and offered him their forgiveness. My parents got me involved in counseling and that was how I learned about Worth Waiting For. I went through training with them and started telling my testimony to other teens. Now I have had the opportunity to tell thousands of others about my secondary virginity and how God has forgiven me.

Things changed really soon after that with Steve. He decided to break up with me and started telling all kinds of lies to our friends at school. He would swear at me and tell me that he never loved me. It was terrible to have to go to school and see him every day. That was the worst part.

That was six years ago. I am now going to a Christian college and my life is very different. I have committed myself to a courtship relationship with any future boyfriend. I believe that I have a bright future, and I thank my mom for having the courage that day to ask the hard question. If she had not confronted me and got me started in counseling, I believe that everything would have worked out very differently. God gave me great parents, and their prayer and love and commitment to me has made all the difference in the world.

How do you feel right after reading Trisha's story?

What does Trisha's story make you want to do?

WHAT WILL HAPPEN IF NOTHING HAPPENS?

What happens to our young people if there is no positive spiritual impact in their lives? Is there any reason to believe that they will feel more secure? Can we expect that they will become less fearful or feel more hopeful? Do you believe that young leaders step up from inside their culture without support and encouragement from caring adults?

The ministries of Worth Waiting For believe in young people and believe that when they are supported and trained and mobilized they can be a strong army for Christ. In order for this to happen we have to do three things well:

We have to do a better job of being informed. We cannot lead them and teach them if we do not know what issues they are going through. You have come a long way toward getting oriented to the issues of sexual health facing teens by going through this book. But just being better informed is not enough.

We have to do a better job of being involved in their lives. We have to take the time to learn about their classes, to listen to their music, to learn the last names of the friends. We will prove our love for them by being in their world and earning their trust. Listen to their band recitals; watch their color guard competitions. That is what this book is all about. But even being informed and involved is still not enough.

We have to do a better job of praying. Information and involvement are great, but without the power and strength of the Holy Spirit, we are sending our children out like sheep to the wolves. God will protect and prepare his children to stand firm in faith and flee immorality. Our job is to pray courageously!

The Baby Boomer Timeline VS The Millenialist Timeline

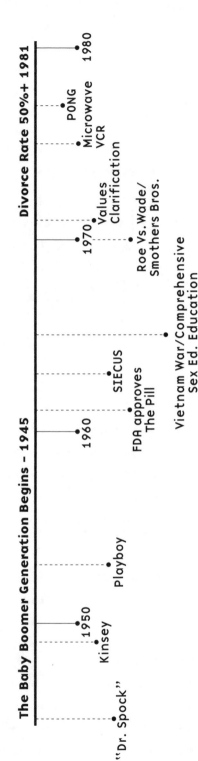

The Baby Boomer Generation Begins – 1945

Divorce Rate 50%+ 1981

"Dr. Spock"

1950

Kinsey

Playboy

1960

FDA approves
The Pill

SIECUS

Vietnam War/Comprehensive
Sex Ed. Education

1970

Values
Clarification

Roe Vs. Wade/
Smothers Bros.

PONG

Microwave
VCR

1980

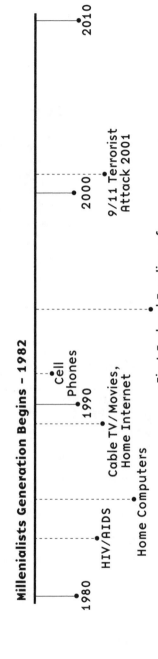

Millenialists Generation Begins – 1982

1980

HIV/AIDS

Home Computers

Cable TV/Movies,
Home Internet

1990

Cell
Phones

First Federal Funding of
Abstinence Sex Education in the U.S.

2000

9/11 Terrorist
Attack 2001

2010

sex education: the surprising Facts

It was the worst day of my life.

My daughter called me about 11:30 Tuesday morning on my cell phone. It was April 20, 1999. In a desperate voice she cried "Daddy, where are you? You have to come home. Have you heard? My friends are dying at Columbine." The words came out with so many tears I could barely understand her. She said it again as I listened, incredulous, unable to believe the words Heather spoke.

"There are people with guns and hand grenades. I have heard that maybe over 100 have been killed. Daddy, get home and go to Columbine. You have to help."

I sped home, throwing caution to the wind. I knew dozens of students from Columbine. While my daughter was a junior at Chatfield, the rival high school to Columbine, many of her closest friends were at Columbine. We live just three miles from the campus and between my daughter's friends and our church, I knew about 50 teens who attended Columbine. I was 60 miles away at the time Heather called and I can remember wondering, "Why are people driving so slow? Don't they know I need to be somewhere?"

I had the radio on and the story was breaking as I drove. The details were unclear, but Heather's story was essentially true. Students were murdering students at Columbine High School.

For the next several hours I was with students and parents trying to make sense of the mayhem. Students I barely knew were hugging me and weeping inconsolably. Dan narrowly missed being shot as he ran from the front doors. Elsie watched as her best friend was killed. Cathy cried and said she knew who it was and frantically asked if I would help her get to the police.

Josh, Cassie and Rachael were missing. I spent the evening with parents waiting at a nearby grade school. We waited as police slowly made their way through the campus freeing students and teachers holed up in classrooms and closets. Earlier in the day, hundreds of teens had sought safety by hiding with friends, adding to the confusion. It was impossible to know who was safe and who was lost. By midnight, all the buses were in and all the missing were accounted for. Josh was on the last bus, to the relief and unspeakable joy of his parents.

For Cassie and Rachael's parents there was untold loss. As bus after bus emptied, the girls never showed. I sat with these parents as best I could, finding myself uncharacteristically silent; not knowing what to say.

It was the worst day of my life.

Dylan Klebold and Eric Harris stormed the Columbine campus and, according to their own notes, exacted a revenge on Columbine for the teasing they had endured while attending there. Thirteen were murdered and then Dylan and Eric took their own lives. Hundreds of others were seriously injured and traumatized. It is all still a mystery, after years of searching and researching. Why?

And for what purpose?

Did we learn anything from this terrible event?

There are several things we *should* have learned.

1. We live in a world of lies and these lies kill.

The lives of those you love depend on understanding that we live in a world of lies. To believe in those lies is to tempt death. Some of the lies are relatively easy to expose. "Money will bring me happiness." "Being popular will make me important." "Being thin will make me beautiful." "Going to church will 'save me,'" and the list goes on.

Dylan and Eric believed a lie. They believed that hate and anger and violence were the answer to their own hurt. They believed that no one loved them enough to make a difference in their lives. They believed that the world is evil and they decided to participate in that evil.

We live in a world of lies and these lies kill. Life is not a game!

2. Our world is not safe.

We've come to believe that schools are safe, churches are safe, shopping malls are safe, next-door neighbors are safe. Not true. Whatever protective factors existed in these once safer places have vanished in a world where violence is commonplace and common friendships have grown to be uncommon.

We live in a fallen world where the prince of the power of the air temporarily has access to lie, murder and steal hearts, lives and souls. Because we live in a world of lies and the world is no longer safe, we as parents must be diligent. We cannot let down our guard. The lives we love depend on our vigilance.

3. Three or Four Degrees Can Turn a Life Around.

Sometimes we believe that people engaging in high risk behavior should do an immediate and abrupt "about face." Most of us don't do that. We don't turn 180 degrees. We turn in small increments at a time. Peer pressure and bad habits tempt us even when we have the best of intentions. Sometimes "turning around" involves huge sacrifices of friendships and activities. Changing is not that easy.

But we as caregivers should remember that we are around for the long haul. We are there to put our arms around our teens and lead them in a new direction. We need to stay with them while they disconnect from the risky behavior and get connected to the healthy behavior. It is a process—more a marathon than a sprint. If you come alongside at-risk youth (and all youth qualify as at-risk!) and move them three degrees with the commitment to stay with them for the remainder of the 177 degrees, you've made a good start. Celebrate and affirm each small step. Small successes pave the way for more success to follow.

WHAT DOES COLUMBINE HAVE TO DO WITH TALKING ABOUT SEX?

Every tragedy that claims the lives of teens is one too many. The Columbine tragedy shook up the country and changed the way many of us look at the world, especially teens. It was a public event with media coverage. But it's not the only kind of tragedy that teenagers face. Misinformation about sex, love and relationships is changing our kids' lives forever—sometimes killing them. Every day, hundreds of babies are aborted, thousands of teens get an incurable STD and too many are coerced into an acts of intimacy they don't want. Young people are dying violently from the inside out. The lessons we learned at Columbine hold true for sex, love and relationships. We live in a world of lies that kill. Our world is not safe. Three or four degrees can turn a life around.

Many parents rely on sex education in the schools, either because they haven't gotten around to talking with their kids or they're afraid to. The problem is we make assumptions about what the school's sex education program is telling our kids based on what we think it should say. The gap between expectations and reality can be huge. Parents who understand the research behind many sex education programs are rightfully alarmed.

WHO IS ALFRED KINSEY AND WHY IS HE RUINING MY CHILDREN?

What most influences our views on sexuality today?

If we asked that question of a group of adults or teens, most would reply TV, movies, magazines, Internet and other forms of media. Most people, youth or adults, would never name a man by the name of Alfred Kinsey. They wouldn't even recognize his name. Yet perhaps more than any other single person in the history of our country, Alfred Kinsey has influenced our cultural and personal views regarding sexuality.

So who is this man and how did he influence our society in such a significant manner? Alfred Kinsey was born in Hoboken, New Jersey in 1894. He was educated at Bowdoin College and Harvard University. Following graduation from Harvard he joined the faculty of Indiana

Kinsey's research was largely accepted as the basis

for the development of sex education in public schools.

But what if the research is incorrect and invalid?

University as a professor of zoology in 1929. He was a worldwide authority regarding the taxonomy of gall wasps. In 1942, Kinsey founded the Institute for Sex Research to investigate human sexual behavior.

It does seem like a far stretch for a scientist to move from entomology to the study of human sexual behavior. In 1997 James H. Jones published a definitive biography of Alfred Kinsey. Jones answers the question as to how this move in interest from entomology to sexual behavior occurred.

> Why had Kinsey cared so passionately and worked so hard all those years? The answer lies in his private life, in the fearful things he had kept hidden from the world. Kinsey was a man with secrets, a man whose stupendous guilt had combined with his puritan work ethic to produce his shameful secrets: he was both a homosexual and a masochist. He had not asked to be either, and he had spent his life deeply conflicted on both accounts. Yet Kinsey understood firsthand how difficult it was to change, and he knew better than to expect sympathy or understanding from society. In order to help himself, he would have to help others. Thus, his messianic crusade to reform the world that oppressed him.[1]

As Kinsey began to form conclusions in his crusade, a number of themes emerged. Several of these themes tried to normalize pedophilia.

This view is evident in Alfred C. Kinsey's *Sexual Behavior in the Human Male,* published in 1948, which created a doctrine of "child sexuality" from data derived from the systematic molestation of hundreds of boys. Kinsey concluded that children are "sexual beings" from birth. In 1953, his companion volume, *Sexual Behavior in the Human Female,* stated, "It is difficult to understand why a child, except for its cultural conditioning, should be disturbed at having its genitals touched."[2]

Kinsey's research was largely accepted as the basis for the development of sex education in public schools throughout the United States until fairly recently. If we accept Kinsey's research as valid, then our current methods and concepts that our students are taught in sex education would be correct.

But what if the research is *incorrect* and *invalid?*

Focus on the Family defines this dilemma we find ourselves in even further.

Fifty years ago, Dr. Alfred C. Kinsey shocked the world with *Sexual Behavior in the Human Male,* followed by *Sexual Behavior in the Human Female.* These "studies" known as the Kinsey Reports, became the basis for sex education from University on down. Kinsey made several bold assertions:

- Traditional sexual morality is worthless
- All sexual activity is natural
- 10% of the population is homosexual
- Children are 'sexual from birth'

Though criticized by some for their sloppy methods, the reports were popularized by the media and have since become unquestioningly accepted by sex educators. Hidden among Kinsey's tables and graphs were horrifying questions:

- How was a 5-month old capable of "multiple orgasms?"
- Who caused a 4-year old to have "26 orgasms in 24 hours?"

Dr. Judith Riesman began asking these questions in the early 1980s. She was outraged by what she found: Pedophiles had been used as "researchers," systematically abusing children, and their detailed records were treated as science by the Kinsey team.[3]

So many outrageous research techniques were used that Kinsey's research in total has been questioned. Yet we base our "safer sex" education on his research.

Another theme that has appeared in Kinsey's work is his anti-Christian sentiment.

There is abundant reason for placing the break-down of our modern home at the door of the Christian Church," he declared. Through its relentless hostility to passion and its strident efforts to control sexual behavior, Christianity was responsible for creating "psychic conflicts" of such magnitude as to constitute probably the most serious threat against the home." Indeed, Kinsey considered the church the family's worst enemy.[4]

What about the research and conclusions of Alfred Kinsey do you find most troubling?

Some people think that Kinsey's research is so old that it is no longer a relevant factor in our culture. What do you think about that?

We must not underestimate the magnitude of this scientist's "research" and its resulting effects on our sexuality education system. Let's take a look at how Kinsey began to influence our educational system far after his death in 1956.

COMPREHENSIVE SEX EDUCATION

The founding organization of comprehensive sex education was and still is the Sex Information and Education Council of the United States (SIECUS). It was founded as an arm of the Kinsey Institute in 1964. It is not a governmental agency but often is mistaken for one because of its name. In the 1960s the Playboy Foundation made an initial grant to establish an office of research services for SIECUS. In 1964, Mary Calderone left her 11-year position as the medical director of Planned Parenthood World Population to become the first director of SIECUS. Remember that Planned Parenthood is famous for contraceptives and abortions on demand without parental consent. In 1968, Hugh Hefner's "Playboy Advisor" column recommended SIECUS sex education to parents. Then in 1970, SIECUS returned the favor and included *The Playboy Philosophy* written by Hugh Hefner on its book list.

Schools set educational guidelines for different school subjects. For instance, there are guidelines for math and different guidelines for science. These guidelines are meant to tell professionals in the educational system what children are supposed to know at a particular age and in particular subjects. There are guidelines for sexuality education also. Comprehensive sex education guidelines for kindergarten through 12th grade were sent to all U.S. school boards in 1991. These guidelines were and still are written by SIECUS.

I was speaking at a Worth Waiting For Teen Leadership Retreat. Twenty-five high school juniors and seniors were taking in my lesson on the SEICUS guidelines. I expected them to patiently endure this somewhat abstract teaching. I was astounded by their reaction. They were not just angry, they were incensed! "Finally," they remarked, "somebody has explained to me why I got so upset in my stomach when they taught us this stuff in high school. This stuff is a lie."

LINDA'S STORY

"The part I really hate is that they are teaching these things to my little sister and little brother. Things that they do not need to know for years, if they ever need to know it. This teaching is destroying my friends. We have to change this!" They finally saw it and they wanted to change it!

ABSTINENCE UNTIL MARRIAGE EDUCATION

What's the rationale for teaching sex education in public schools? It's generally accepted by educators, administrators and parents that it's a good thing for children to have a basic understanding of how the systems of the body work. The purpose is to increase healthy behaviors while decreasing unhealthy behaviors.

We see that concept clearly in drug education. Educators teach children the harmful and sometimes devastating effects of the use of illegal substances and how to avoid pressure to use them. This is usually seen as good educational practice.

Another basic premise that comprehensive sex education supports is that teaching condom education in the public schools will result in a decrease in teen pregnancy and in the incidence of sexually transmitted diseases (STDs). However, after years of comprehensive sex education, the outcome was the opposite. Teen pregnancy rates began to climb dramatically in the 1970s and STDs became more prevalent and more diseases emerged in the sexually active population. This change gained the attention of many health educators and health professionals.

In 1992, a summit was held in Washington, D.C. to investigate and discuss alternatives to current sex education in public schools. Something was wrong, that much was clear.

Teen pregnancy and STDs were steadily rising and it seemed as though sex was becoming recreation rather than an act of love in marriage. In that same year Dr. Joe McIlhaney established The Medical Institute for Sexual Health (MISH). This was a quiet development, but one of the most important to the practice of "abstinence until marriage education." Dr. McIlhaney, an obstetrician and gynecologist, was seeing many young patients in his practice devastated by the twin epidemics of teen pregnancy and sexually transmitted disease. "Driven by medical, educational and other scientific data, The Medical Institute informs, educates and provides solutions to medical professionals, educators, government officials, parents and the media about problems associated with sexually transmitted disease and nonmarital pregnancy."[5]

Also in 1992, Dr. Judith Reisman wrote her book entitled *Kinsey, Sex and Fraud.* The purpose of this book was to uncover the unscientific nature of the research of Alfred Kinsey. This sent shockwaves through the ranks of health educators, causing many to realize that the rationale for modern sex education might be seriously flawed. Curricula that were more than traditional sex education emerged in the marketplace. This included the concept of saving sex until marriage to truly prevent out-of-wedlock births and to stop the spread of sexually transmitted diseases. Along with the new curricula came the launch of numerous non-profit organizations that were specifically designed to develop, teach and train an entirely new paradigm for sexuality education.

In 1996, two landmark developments occurred. The Medical Institute for Sexual Health published a second set of sexuality education guidelines. This is the first time that an alternative set of guidelines was offered for public school administrators and teachers. The new guidelines were titled *National Guidelines for Sexuality and Character Education.*

The other landmark development in 1996 was the passing of the Federal Welfare Reform Law. This was the first time that our national government passed legislation to give money for abstinence until marriage education. This law initially allocated $50 million for each fiscal year from 1998–2002. Currently our federal government is allocating $50 million for abstinence until marriage education through Title V funds[6] and $30 million in 2003 in monies called SPRANS grants (Special Projects of Regional and National Significance).[7]

What kind of sex education guidelines are being used in your child's public or private school, SIECUS or MISH guidelines?

If you don't know, what would it take to find out?

Who at your school sets the policy on the school's guidelines for sex education?

Are your schools open to parental involvement? Why so or why not?

What kinds of thoughts come to your mind when you think of introducing an abstinence-until-marriage program involving teens you know? How do you think they would need to be approached in order for them to be receptive?

MORE ABOUT GUIDELINES

Guidelines for various subjects are not in themselves a curriculum. Guidelines are tools for school administrators and teachers to establish appropriate learning standards for a unique age level in a particular subject. They can be very subjective. Let's compare the guidelines issued by SIECUS and the Medical Institute for Sexual Health.

Both are written for kindergarten through 12th grade, and the learning categories are similar. One category is human development. Let's look at the guidelines for ages five to eight to understand the differences in content. According to the Guidelines for Comprehensive Sexuality Education[8] from SIECUS, during this age and in the first subcategory of reproductive anatomy and physiology:

- Each body part has a correct name and a specific function.
- A person's genitals, reproductive organs and genes determine whether the person is male or female.
- Boys and men have a penis, scrotum and testicles.
- Girls and women have a vulva, clitoris, vagina, uterus and ovaries.
- Both girls and boys have body parts that feel good when touched.

Within this document the subcategory states, "The human body has the capability to reproduce as well as to give and receive sexual pleasure." What we begin to see is a concept of masturbation and explicit anatomy lessons all the way down to the kindergarten level. This particular set of guidelines can also be interpreted to be a subtle normalizing of pedophilia. Boys and girls (not men and women) have body parts that feel good when touched. If there are no moral constraints put on this discussion, pedophilia, which was "normalized" by Kinsey, follows. This outrages many adults. But let's go onto the subcategory of reproduction. The developmental messages for five to eight year olds include:

- Reproduction requires both a man and a woman.
- Men and women have reproductive organs that enable them to have a child.
- Men and women have specific cells in their bodies that enable them to reproduce.
- Not all men and women decide to have children.

- When a woman is pregnant, the fetus grows inside her body in her uterus.
- Babies usually come out of a woman's body through an opening called a vagina.
- Some babies are born by an operation call a Caesarian Section.
- Women have breasts that can provide milk for a baby.
- Vaginal intercourse occurs when a man and a woman place the penis inside the vagina.

Within this document the subcategory states, "Most people have both the capability and the ability to choose to reproduce." We see a description of the action of vaginal intercourse. Remember, some of the children this is aimed at are five years old. This begs the question: what kindergartner needs to know explicitly about vaginal intercourse? Is this an appropriate topic to teach our very young children?

Let's look at one more category for ages five to eight, the topic of sexual identity and orientation. According to the guidelines from SIECUS these are the developmental messages that our children of this age are to learn.

- Everyone is born a boy or a girl.
- Boys and girls grow up to be men and women.
- Human beings experience different kinds of loving.
- Most men and women are heterosexual, which means they will be attracted to and fall in love with someone of the other gender.
- Some men and women are homosexual, which means they will be attracted to and fall in love with someone of the same gender.
- Homosexuals are also known as gay men and lesbian women.

Already, in the first guidelines for kindergartners we are introducing the concept of gay and lesbian relationships. (You can view the entire document of SIECUS guidelines on the website: http://www.siecus.org/pubs.)

The Medical Institute for Sexual Health guidelines are a character-building set of sexuality guidelines that differ greatly from the SIECUS guidelines. If sexual self-control is a value that we hold for our children and ourselves, then we must develop the character qualities necessary for self-control. The MISH guidelines are built on four components: character education, skills for abstinence, information and family life. Character education is seen as a necessary quality for developing healthy relationships. "It also encourages young people to develop such traits as generosity, compassion, justice, courage, sound judgment, kindness, honesty, moderation and self-control."[9] Skills for abstinence are an essential component to these guidelines, because it does take skill to deal with a society that is saturated by sexual messages and remain abstinent. A few examples of the important skills are refusal skills, male-female relationship skills and responding to media pressure.

Information is another essential component to these guidelines. Our young people need and deserve accurate facts about a full range of issues relating to sexual health and sexuality. Family life is the fourth component, and perhaps it's the most important. Research is showing time and time again that teens who feel loved and included in special family relationships abstain from high-risk behaviors. And parents are the primary sex educators of their children. Teens listen when they are told family values. This may seem hard to believe, but research shows that it's true!

Let's look at MISH categories that correspond to the SEICUS These are also for children who are the ages five to eight. The topics covered in this section are human body and health, reproduction, puberty, gender roles and stages of life. Following are the MISH guidelines in this category.

- Girls and boys need to care for their bodies.
- Human babies develop inside their mothers.
- Human babies are best cared for by loving and mature parents with support from other responsible adults.
- Boys and girls are similar in some ways and different in other ways.
- Throughout childhood, a person grows physically, intellectually, emotionally, socially, spiritually and morally.

There is a vast difference in information and values in these guidelines than the previous set. The emphasis is on the importance of parents raising a child. There is no blatant anatomy and physiology

If sexual self-control is a value that we hold for our children and ourselves, then we must develop the character qualities necessary for self-control.

lesson for the very young elementary student. These guidelines acknowledge that we grow in all different ways including the physical, intellectual, emotional, social, spiritual and moral aspects.

Another corresponding set of guidelines has to do with body appreciation and human sexuality, sexual urges and desires, lifelong commitment and fidelity. Again we will look at the five to eight year old category.

- Developing a habit of self-control can help us manage our desires and urges.
- Family members show intimacy by affectionate actions and loving words.
- Family life is the first experience a person has in understanding the meaning of commitment.

The focus of this material is on self-control and the importance of families. The core values of love, family affection and commitment are all there to make the world a safe place in which to grow. (You can purchase the entire set of Medical Institute guidelines through their website at www.medinstitute.org/products/index.htm.)

DOES THE SITUATION MATTER?

We've talked a great deal about the history, guidelines and basic differences between comprehensive sex education and abstinence until marriage education. The SIECUS guidelines are meant to drive the philosophy and values of comprehensive sex education. The Medical Institute guidelines are meant to drive the philosophy and values of abstinence until marriage. But what about sexuality education in our Christian homes, schools and churches? What are the differences in character-based sex education as seen in the MISH guidelines, and Christ-centered sex education?

Character-based education is passing on values and behaviors that are deemed critical for the good of society. Think of it like the Boy Scout Key Beliefs: "A Scout is Trustworthy, Loyal, Helpful, Friendly, Courteous, Kind, Obedient, Cheerful, Thrifty, Clean and Reverent." This is a great list of desirable character traits, and character education seeks to develop standards like this. They appeal to certain traditional "agreed upon" values and beliefs. Generally, we count on parents and family to pass these values on, generation to generation. For years, character-education was a cornerstone of our schools, clubs and service groups. Then something began to change.

In the 60s and 70s a new philosophy began to creep into our schools, an idea often called Situational Ethics, pioneered by Joseph Fletcher (1905-1991). His work, *Situation Ethics*, founded the modern situational ethics movement. Since then, almost every publication on situational ethics has referred to the model presented in Fletcher's writings. Fletcher was an Episcopal priest, a member of the Euthanasia Educational Counsel, and an advocate for Planned Parenthood. He was a supporter of both euthanasia and abortion.

According to Fletcher's model, he states that decision-making should be based upon the circumstances of a particular situation, and not upon fixed Law. His only absolute is Love.

"Love should be the motive behind every decision. As long as Love is your intention, the end justifies the means. Justice is not in the letter of the Law, it is in the distribution of Love."

Fletcher's model of Situational Ethics appears reasonable upon a glance, yet given careful consideration, its flaw becomes apparent. Situational Ethics is based upon "God is Love" in 1 John 4:8. However, in the very next chapter we read, "This is the love of God, that we keep His commandments. And His commandments are not burdensome" (1 John 5:3). While Fletcher holds that any commandment may be broken in good conscience if Love is one's intention, the Bible states that the keeping of God's commandments is loving God. "Situational Ethics" is supposedly based upon the Bible, yet it contradicts the Bible.[10]

The concept of "situational ethics" became the foundation for comprehensive sex education. The SIECUS guidelines are built on ideas consistent with values that "flex" situation-to-situation, based on how "emotionally ready" I feel or how "in love" I may think I am. Hard or

**Character-based education confronts the situation
ethics of comprehensive sex education. Parents are lifted
up as the main authority in a child's life.**

absolute standards of morality are rejected as too harsh and antiquated. The church is considered to be restrictive and parental considerations are clearly optional.

In contrast, character-based sex education confronts the situational ethics of comprehensive sex education. Parents are lifted up as the main authority figures in a child's life, but values are usually based on social research of current cultural values. These are public opinion polls of prevailing thoughts. While most of us treasure values of self-discipline and sacrificial love, without strong absolute values even character-based education is open for interpretation. This creates a dilemma for character-based sex education proponents. Who defines the most desirable character traits and which traits are most important?

Morals and values are softly suggested in character-based sex education. These are not intended to be absolutes as there is little tolerance of absolutes in today's school systems. The focus of this type of sex education is on measurable behavior, in order to make sure that goals and objectives are being obtained. And since these behaviors are measured in the school classroom, these goals are focused on public behaviors. It is about performance of the individual. How well the child or teen makes good decisions determines his or her success.

WHAT'S A PARENT TO DO?

What do parents need to do to make good decisions about a child attending sex education classes? If children or teens are in public schools, parents should have the opportunity to "opt out" their children from sex education. This means that parents can tell the principal and teacher that their child is not allowed to attend the class and alternative activities should be provided. Some school systems have an "opt in" choice for parents. This is a way to make sure that all parents give permission for their children to attend the classes.

It's up to you to determine whether the sex education classes taught in your child's school are good and helpful. Here is a set of questions to ask a school principal as soon as the class is announced.

- What is the name of the curriculum?
- When can I look at the curriculum? (Look for themes of homosexuality, masturbation, sexual activity outside of marriage, the concept that readiness for sex is determined by each individual and abortion.)
- How did you choose this particular curriculum?
- Did you use a set of guidelines to determine which curriculum to use? And if so, what set of guidelines was used by you or the school district?
- Are there videos that will be shown?
- When can I view the videos?
- When is the parent orientation night? If there isn't one planned, volunteer to help set one up.
- Are parents allowed to attend the class(es) with the students?
- Will you provide the parents with a list of topics that will be covered during each class session?
- Will there be interactive homework given so that we, as parents, can talk to our children about our values and morals regarding what is being taught?
- What will my child do during the time of the class(es) if we decide not to include him or her in this course?

SEX EDUCATION IN THE IMAGE OF CHRIST

Christ-centered sex education is based on two shaping concepts: absolute truth and understanding that God is looking for a special kind of obedience to that truth. This obedience is governed not just by outward behavior, but our hearts and motives as well. You will remember that Jesus raised the standard for goodness. A man with lust or anger in his heart is as guilty of murder and adultery as the one who actually commits the physical act (Matthew 5:27). In Christ-centered sex education, the Bible is the final authority on acceptable behavior. Science can be an excellent tool for research and proving God's creation and truth, but science, especially the social sciences, are based on public opinion and bias that is always changing. We continually discover new "truths" that disprove yesterday's "truth." But the authentic truth of the Bible never changes.

Let's use the chart below to contrast the ideas of character-based sex education and Christ-centered sex education.

Character-Based Sex Education	Christ-Centered Sex Education
Sociological and Psychological	Spiritual and Biblical
Traditional Authorities	Final Authority
"Good of Many"	"Kingdom Good"
Based on Social Research	Based on a Biblical Mandate
Changes Over Time	Never Changes
Moral "Suggestions"	Moral "Absolutes"
Focus on Measurable Behavior	Focus on Motives and Attitudes
Only Public Behavior Matters	Public and Private Behavior Matter
All About Observable Behaviors	Motives of the Heart
Supremacy of Mankind	Lordship of Christ
Educational and Medical	Relational and Spiritual
How Close to the Edge Can I Get?	Where Does God Want Me to Stand?
Freedom From …	Freedom To …

Character-based sex education has its limits. It cannot rely on ultimate authority, only traditional authorities. These have changed though the years. The phrase "traditional American values" doesn't imply the same thing it did 100 years ago.

Don't misunderstand these comparisons. Character-based education is the best the world can offer. It is far better than comprehensive, condom-based sex education. However, any time we leave God out of the equation, we are presenting only part of the truth, and the part we are leaving out is the most important piece. In our public schools, the best we can do right now is character-based sex education. But in our homes and our churches, we can tell the whole truth. Character-based sex education tends to focus on measurable behavior, trying to answer the question "How far can I go?" with the most current medical, psychological or cultural "norms."

Christ-centered sex education provides the key spiritual component that's missing in other programs. Christ-centered sex education recognizes that choices of lifestyle and sexuality are acts of will and character. Those led by this philosophy are as concerned for our private decisions as they are for outward behavior others can measure. Character-based sex education threatens to be consumed with "avoiding the worst," freedom from disease and broken-heartedness. Christ-centered education is about "having the best," like an intimate marriage marked by trust and satisfaction, with the freedom to experience fearless love without shame, guilt or doubt.

CHRIST-CENTERED HEALTH

Scripture celebrates the whole person concept of mental and physical health. It discourages us from compartmentalized thinking. It speaks to the truth of the individual's need to be integrated and whole. It also communicates beautifully the way all of us in the Body of Christ are fitted together to honor the Father.

> *The body is a unit, though it is made up of many parts; and though all its parts are many, they form one body. So it is with Christ. For we were all baptized by one Spirit into one body—whether Jews or Greeks, slave or free—and we were all given the one Spirit to drink.*

Now the body is not made up of one part but of many. If the foot should say, "Because I am not a hand, I do not belong to the body," it would not for that reason cease to be part of the body. And if the ear should say, "Because I am not an eye, I do not belong to the body," it would not for that reason cease to be part of the body. If the whole body were an eye, where would the sense of hearing be? If the whole body were an ear, where would the sense of smell be? But in fact God has arranged the parts in the body, every one of them, just as he wanted them to be. If they were all one part, where would the body be? As it is, there are many parts, but one body.

The eye cannot say to the hand, "I don't need you!" And the head cannot say to the feet, "I don't need you!" On the contrary, those parts of the body that seem to be weaker are indispensable, and the parts that we think are less honorable we treat with special honor. And the parts that are unpresentable are treated with special modesty, while our presentable parts need no special treatment. But God has combined the members of the body and has given greater honor to the parts that lacked it, so that there should be no division in the body, but that its parts should have equal concern for each other. If one part suffers, every part suffers with it; if one part is honored, every part rejoices with it.

Now you are the body of Christ, and each one of you is a part of it (1 Corinthians 12:12–27).

Every part of who we are is connected with others. Consider the way this chart puts it:

Dimensions of the Christ-Centered Life and Health

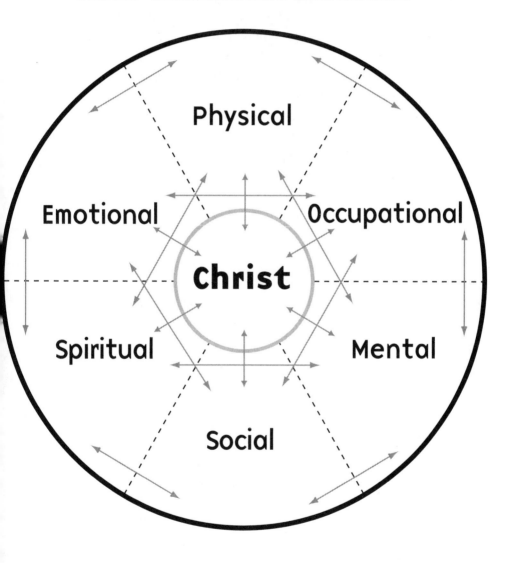

Notice that in this model the spiritual isn't just one of the compartments on the edge of our life. The spiritual part of who we are should touch every area of our life. Theologians call this the Lordship of Christ. When he has access to and control of all parts of who I am, he has true Lordship of my life. Though our body is made of many parts, at the center of my life is the person of Jesus Christ, my own personal Alpha and Omega. When I have Jesus as my centering truth, it is so much easier to distinguish a lie from the truth. From the center, Jesus can help keep me in balance and whole. He sits on the throne of my life and commands me

The physical, emotional, sexual and spiritual health of our children depends on our ability to live and communicate this truth. Let's not give up, for we are promised a reward if we do not grow faint in doing good! (Galatians 6:9.)

confront
●THE
Lies

Early in this book we made the case that we live in a world of lies. These lies penetrate every aspect of our lives and sometimes come from the most unexpected sources. If the lies always came from people we distrust, it would be easier to sort them out. But the sad truth is, sometimes our best friends and loved ones tell us the lies. Not that they mean to! The motive to deceive may not exist. But the telling of an untruth, even with the best of motives, can have the same devastating effect as telling a boldface lie.

This is especially true of trusted adults. When we get our information wrong, don't pay close enough attention or even offer an unsubstantiated educated guess, we can destroy teens who trust us to counsel them on issues of sexual health and love. Teens hear lies all the time in school, from their friends, even at times from family and church. Bad information given with good intention is still bad information.

Eight primary lies are prevalent in our culture. There are, of course, variations of these lies that are equally dangerous. (If you want to get a longer more detailed look at these lies that deceive our youth, check out *Fearless Love,* another book in the Worth Waiting For series.)

Let's take a look at these the lies and be ready to correct them and clarify God's truth for our kids.

LIE #1: SEX IS BAD

One lie that can confuse us as we try to understand intimacy and our sexuality is the sense that sex is dirty, bad or shameful.

This message often comes from the conservative church culture, where embarrassed parents that find it hard to talk about sex. A child or teen asks a simple question and instead of getting a simple answer hears, "We'll talk about that later," or "Ask your mom or dad," or "Don't ever mention that word in this house," or some kind of lame run-around answer. Many parents have a hard time talking about sex because they feel ashamed about their own past or because the intense intimacy of the subject is just plain intimidating. Let's face it, we joke around about sex, but honest, open conversations about sexuality don't seem to happen anywhere except on MTV. So kids get the impression that sex is shameful or dirty.

When God created man and woman, he designed them in his own image. In the Garden of Eden, before they disobeyed God, Adam and Eve were naked and not ashamed. God designed us from the start to enjoy our sexuality with our partners *without shame!* When Adam and Eve ate the forbidden fruit, everything changed.

Somewhere along the line, Christians came to think of the pleasures of the body as anti-spiritual. In truth, Jesus, Paul the Apostle and the Scriptures as a whole have a grand view of sex when enjoyed according to God's design, in the context of a covenant marriage relationship. Sex in marriage is a gift to celebrate, excellent in every way.

God designed sex to be enjoyed in marriage because he wanted us to enjoy the fullest expression of this intimate act of love. He wanted us to have abundant life and fearless love. In marriage, trust and commitment make it possible to enjoy each other and to raise children without fear, doubt, guilt, shame and the threat of disease and emotional tragedy.

Look up the following verses, then write what you think God is saying about sex, love and relationships.

Genesis 2:25

Song of Solomon 5:1; 6:3, 8

Matthew 19:6

Ephesians 5:21–32

1 Corinthians 7:3

LIE #2: SEX IS LOVE AND LOVE IS SEX

Watching shows like "The Orange County" and soap operas, noticing the so-called family magazines at the supermarket, we begin to recognize a theme of what society says about sex. One of the lies that the media projects is that "sex is love and love is sex." It seems there is virtually no difference between the two. Love can mean almost anything, and sex is just one more way getting a physical "rush." Sex is not all that different from climbing a mountain or driving a fast car.

Let's look at it this way: Is it possible to have love without sex? The obvious answer is yes. We have various kinds of love relationships all the time without them turning sexual. The Greek language does a great job of helping us differentiate the different kinds of love. There is *Storge* or family love, the kind of love a mother has for her child and

Phileo, the love that best friends share. There is *Eros,* the sexual kind of attraction and *Agape,* sacrificial love that seems to be harder to find. So there are four kinds of love, only one of which becomes sexual in healthy relationships, *Eros.* And according to God's design, expressions of *Eros* or erotic love are reserved for marriage alone.

You can have love without sex, but what about sex without love? Sadly, we see this explicitly played out all the time. Prostitution, Internet porn, "Hooking Up" are all expressions of sex without love. When the terms "love" and "sex" become synonymous, a dangerous lie forms. Young girls have been trapped by the line, "If you loved me you would want to meet my needs." This is a taking, selfish, imitation love and has all the fingerprints of Satan.

Don't let your children believe this dangerous deception.

LIE #3: SEX IS AN OBLIGATION

Dear Abby,

I am having a tough time making up my mind about something and I was hoping you could help.

Here is what's going on. I am dating this guy and I really like him. It is the first time I have gone steady, and he is really important to me. We have been going out for almost three months and I think that I am really in love. He's a little old (19) and I'm a little young (I'll be 14 in a month), but he is really nice.

The problem is that he is really putting on the pressure to have sex. He keeps trying to get me alone and then he starts putting a move on me. I keep telling him to stop, but he says that if I love him, I would have sex with him. I am afraid of what might happen with AIDS and all. He tells me that all his friends are having sex, but I don't know a single friend of mine that has gone all the way.

He has spent a lot of money on me and takes me out to eat and stuff. We are planning on going to the Prom this spring and he says it's time for me to pay him back, and that if I really loved him I would be willing to meet his needs. He wants to get a hotel room after Prom.

I know that if my parents found out I had sex they would kill me. They don't even know that I'm going out with someone. And besides I don't really want to yet. But I am afraid he will leave me.

I don't think I want it to start out this way, but I don't want to lose him. I hope you can help me because I am really,

Confused in Colorado

The lie that sex is an obligation is obvious in this letter. It's pretty easy to get mad at the young man. But in real life, a guy or girl saying, "I'll leave you if you don't put out" is a pretty intimidating situation. This is what is called "coerced sex." It is the idea that because someone spends a lot of money on dinner and a date or dance, sex is required as a "payback" for the evening. This is a lie and the moral equivalent of emotional rape.

Sex never is an obligation, not even in marriage. Even in marriage, it is still a gift of love and never pushes its way in another's life. No *always* means no. No matter how much money a guy spends on a date, no matter what a girl whispers tenderly, a teen who wants to wait until marriage has the right to wait. If sex is the medium of exchange needed to keep the love, then it isn't love!

LIE #4: IT'S MY FAULT

Young children are developmentally unable to process in abstract terms. That means that abstract ideas (like sharing and honesty) are difficult for children to understand. They tend to believe most anything an adult tells them, which is why young children believe in the Easter Bunny and Santa Claus, but older kids figure out the truth. If a parent or adult abuses the child, the child has no perspective about who is at fault. The abuser may tell lies to the child or threaten the child with untruths. It is impossible for the child to understand that it is not his or her fault.

When children are abused or hurt, it is not uncommon for them to say to themselves, "I must have done something wrong to be hurt like this. In some way that I don't understand, this must be my fault." That childlike logic stays with them into adulthood, leading them to believe a terrible lie about themselves. Counselors say that victims of abuse often see themselves as the perpetrator, not the victim. This confusion, this lie, can destroy a person from the inside out. Young women who are victims of date rape may fall prey to the same lie: "I must have done something to deserve it." It could happen to your teen or one of your teen's friends. It may be awkward, but it's important to talk about this kind of injustice. Jesus was steadfast in his resolve to confront injustice. He stood up for the oppressed, and I know that he would be proud to see us confronting these issues.

Our God is a God of hope and a God of power. That means that even in the worst situations, there is hope for healing and forgiveness.

LIE #5: THIS ONLY INVOLVES THE TWO OF US

Consider for a moment the biblical story of David and Bathsheba from 2 Samuel 11–12. David saw a beautiful woman and asked that she be brought to him. They slept together. As a woman subject to the king, Bathsheba may not have felt like she had any choice in the matter. Perhaps David arrogantly thought he could do whatever he wanted. Or maybe Bathsheba knew what she was doing. Either way, they weren't counting on Bathsheba getting pregnant. David tried to make it look like Bathsheba's husband was the father of the child, but Uriah didn't cooperate with David's plan. So David had Uriah killed in battle. Other innocent soldiers were killed. Joab, the military leader, was put in a position of doing something he knew was wrong in order to please the king. God's judgment on David and Bathsheba was the death of their innocent son. David and Bathsheba's lives were changed forever.

Sexual behavior, whether or not a pregnancy results, affects far more people than just the two involved.

LIE #6: I WON'T GET PREGNANT

Many teens have misinformation about how pregnancy can occur. They need the facts. Pregnancy is a big deal, and it's a bigger risk than many teenagers realize.

LIE #7: I WON'T GET A DISEASE

Back when most of us were teenagers there were two main sexually transmitted diseases, gonorrhea and syphilis. Now there are between

25 and 50 sexually transmitted diseases and the number is growing every year. One of the reasons disease is proliferating is that more and more people are having sex outside of marriage.

Sexually transmitted disease is usually in the form of a virus or bacteria, but there are also many forms that do not fall into these two categories. Bacterial infections are treated using antibiotics and are usually curable. However, some strains of bacterial STD, including some forms of gonorrhea, no longer respond to antibiotics.

That's a tough part of STDs—they change as time goes on. STDs are like any other infection. The germs that cause the disease try to stay alive. So, in order to stay alive and not be killed by medication, they change and are unaffected by the antibiotic—smart germs!

LIE #8 I WON'T GET AIDS

Human Immunodeficiency Virus (HIV) was first discussed and named in the public in 1982. Many of us who teach teens today grew up at a time when there was no discussion of HIV and AIDS. Today we are experiencing devastating consequences to individuals, families and whole cultures due to HIV.

In our culture, probably no health concern has drawn more attention than HIV/AIDS over the last 20 years. Millions have died, millions more have been orphaned and millions more infected. Billions of dollars have been spent to find a cure, and yet none is in sight. Even with all this attention, there is still a lot of confusion and misinformation out there. Sadly, the church usually doesn't speak about AIDS. We tend to ignore this terrible killer. By not speaking the truth we participate in the lies and misconceptions.

BACK TO THE BASICS—PARENTING 101

Here are some bullet points on parenting that transcend this subject. If you want to have an honest straightforward conversation with your teens about sex, lay the groundwork for that successful conversation by understanding and sticking to the basics of parenting. See if these ideas look familiar to you. They should. There is nothing all that new about them. But football coaches always seem to get "back to the basics" when there is an important confrontation looming. If you have an important confrontation coming up with your teens then you'd better get back to the basics, too.

• Be a parent first, not a friend first.

We make a mistake when we strive to be a friend to our children first. Our role as stewards of the children that God has given us is to teach and model moral and spiritual truths. We see in Scripture that God takes this very seriously.

> *Hear, O Israel: The Lord our God, the Lord is one. Love the Lord your God with all your heart and with all your soul and with all your strength. These commandments that I give you today are to be upon your hearts. Impress them on your children. Talk about them when you sit at home and when you walk along the road, when you lie down and when you get up. Tie them as symbols on your hands and bind them on your foreheads* (Deuteronomy 6:4–8).

If we start making compromises that bring the children and teenagers in our care to the status of friends, we're quickly tempted to get soft on discipline. We take short cuts and open ourselves to manipulation. Be a parent first. When our children are 25 years old, we can inverse that relationship very naturally.

• Be in their world.

When our children are small they want to be in our world. They want to go fishing with us, not because they really like fishing, but because they want to be with us. They will go out and rake leaves with us, paint the house with us, do the laundry with us, because they want to be with us. As our children develop through the stages of life, they become more independent, find their own friends and hobbies and find activities that they enjoy.

Now it all turns upside down. Now instead of their wanting to be in our world because they want to be with us, we have to be in their world because we want to be with them. We are tempted to pout and argue saying, "Why don't you want to go fishing with me? You always loved to fish. What is the matter with you? You've changed! All you are is a selfish, ungrateful child!" All that has really happened is that they now have their own lives and they used to just have ours. The sacrificial thing to do is to be in their world, learn their music, learn their friends' names, talk about their teachers and don't try to fix everything. Just go with them and demonstrate "Incarnational Love." Do as Jesus did for us—sacrifice and go into their world to prove your love to them.

• Be just, not fair.

Every parent has heard the angry accusation "That's not fair!" Sometimes it makes us laugh, sometimes it makes us angry. Being fair means that everyone gets the same. I get one, you get one. It is not a function of having earned the gift or responsibility or opportunity; it is just the idea that everyone is the same.

The concepts of equality and fairness have somehow been connected in our culture. There is another way of looking at this idea, a better way. The Bible prioritizes a concept called justice. In this scheme, people earn opportunity and responsibility. Some comes initially by age or position, but that privilege can be lost or forsaken by poor behavior. The just way of doing things looks more like Jesus' Parable of the Talents found in Matthew 25. In this story it is made clear that we have to treat what we've been given with respect and stewardship. If we treat our responsibilities well, we can expect more privilege and reward. If we squander our opportunities, even what we have may be taken away. This is justice. Consider making evenhanded justice the trademark of your home or ministry, not simple fairness. It pays off fast!

• Clear communications are a must.

Sometimes we have expectations for our teens that are unspoken. We make the assumption that every thinking human (this may be the problem!) would have the same assumptions. Things like putting away the milk before it gets warm or filling the car up with gas after draining it. Effective parenting anticipates that the average teen has different priorities and values than the average adult. So *before* something bad happens, we clearly share our expectations ("The gas tank is full. Fill it before you bring it home.") and the consequences of what happens when those expectations are not met ("If the tank is not full you cannot use the car Friday night for your date."). Too often we lay down the law, but not the consequence of breaking the law. It is the second half of that equation that affects behavior, not the first half. Plus, sharing all this up front spares us having to invent a punishment after the fact, or being too emotionally involved that we inflict punishments that do not fit the crime ("You are grounded forever!").

• Help them succeed.

Psychologists tell us that we need seven compliments for every one chastisement. The world of teens is hard enough without parents piling on criticism. Every day most teens make thousands of decisions—most of them very good decisions. But because we are not following them around with a video camera and reviewing it later, we tend to see only the bad decisions. Great parenting is a ministry of encouragement and uplifting talk. Just like the management phrase, "Catch your employees doing something right," parents, teachers and youth leaders can employ the same axiom: "Catch your teen doing something right." It shows that you are watching, that you appreciate their efforts to be productive and that you see their character being conformed into the image of Christ. Sometimes we have to really look hard! Teens can get pretty lax when they feel safe, like they might at home or church. All the same, our job is to encourage, not exasperate!

• Trust is earned. Love is given.

Books have been written on this idea. It just seems that either they aren't very good or we don't read them. We are still really confused! Trust and love get mixed up all the time. We say to our teen, "You cannot drive downtown Friday night." And the response is, "You don't love me."

The parents' unspoken understanding is that the car holds only four people and the teen wants to take six friends. The teen in question has had a license for three months, not three years, and has never driven downtown, much less at night. And Friday night downtown is filled with drunks driving around being stupid. The truth is, "As a parent, I love you, but I don't trust you, your friends and this environment."

The teen, on the other hand, is reacting to a world that makes him or her earn love all the time. Unless you are prettier, smarter, funnier, sexier, wealthier, stronger than your peers, you are not loved. The exchange about the car feels like every other exchange—earned love.

According to world values, love is earned and trust is given:

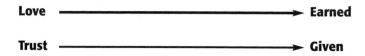

But this is wrong! It is the result of living in a world of lies. According to God's plan for our lives, love is always given, without condition or expectation, even to our enemies. Trust, on the other hand, is earned by responsible behavior, not according to gender, age or position. God's design looks like this:

Help your teens to understand that trust is always earned and love is a gift. Don't let them be deceived by the world into getting it backward!

> **How can you as a as parent help teens understand this critical concept?**

ASKING FOR WISDOM

God has promised us the grace and wisdom to do the hard work of talking to our children about sex.

Consider it pure joy, my brothers, whenever you face trials of many kinds, because you know that the testing of your faith develops per-

severance. Perseverance must finish its work so that you may be mature and complete, not lacking anything. If any of you lacks wisdom, he should ask God, who gives generously to all without finding fault, and it will be given to him. But when he asks, he must believe and not doubt, because he who doubts is like a wave of the sea, blown and tossed by the wind. That man should not think he will receive anything from the Lord; he is a double-minded man, unstable in all he does (James 1:2–8).

God recognizes the profound undertaking he has asked us to perform when it comes to talking to our youth about sex. He, above all others, sees the power in sex. He designed it that way. He knows that this is intimate and personal. That is why he designed us, who know our children best, to do the sharing. Kids are hearing lies all around them; you have the opportunity to help them challenge the lies by giving them the truth. Talking about sex isn't biology, so don't be intimidated that you don't know enough. Thank God we have a Savior who understands our trials and tribulations and gives us wisdom to face the task with courage and resolve and caring.

But be warned! Do not take this responsibility lightly, as some others have done. Having doubts about God's equipping us with wisdom leads us to be open to lies: "Who am I to talk to my child about sex? I made so many mistakes, and there is so much I don't know. Besides, I am so uncomfortable. I am sure the school will do a good enough job. Besides, I learned, kind of."

This "double-minded" thinking is a lie from the heart of Satan. Courage, parent! Stand firm, Pastor! You are your kids' last best hope to navigate these difficult waters without being destroyed. Persevere! Put your plan together today, pray today and start today. It is never too late to be truthful and real. God is on your side. Do not be afraid. He will give you the words. Trust him!

chapter six

MARRIAGE: BEAUTIFUL BY Design

Kids today are growing up in a culture of divorce. They are bombarded by images that devalue God's gift of sex and the sacrificial love that sustains a marriage relationship. Young couples speak vows full of warmth and good intentions, but stop short of "till death parts us." Instead they say something like, "for as long as our love shall last." State after state addresses the question of whether marriage means a man and a woman, or two people regardless of gender. Many denominations offer a service to bless same-sex unions even in states that do not recognize them as legal marriages. Kids get all kinds of ideas of what marriage is and isn't from the news and which parent's house they're sleeping at tonight.

So how do we teach kids God's view of marriage? First, we can't teach what we don't know. So we need to explore what God's Word says about marriage, including the sexual dimension. Second, kids learn far more by watching what we do than listening to what we say. We talk with our lives, not just with our words. So let's take a moment to listen to what we're saying before we ask our kids to do the same.

THE BIBLE ON MARRIAGE

Let's look at some key Bible passages about marriage.

The Lord God said, "It is not good for the man to be alone. I will make a helper suitable for him."

Now the Lord God had formed out of the ground all the beasts of the field and all the birds of the air. He brought them to the man to see what he would name them; and whatever the man called each living creature, that was its name. So the man gave names to all the livestock, the birds of the air and all the beasts of the field.

But for Adam no suitable helper was found. So the Lord God caused the man to fall into a deep sleep; and while he was sleeping, he took one of the man's ribs and closed up the place with flesh. Then the Lord God made a woman from the rib he had taken out of the man, and he brought her to the man.

The man said, "This is now bone of my bones and flesh of my flesh; she shall be called woman, for she was taken out of man."

For this reason a man will leave his father and mother and be united to his wife, and they will become one flesh.

The man and his wife were both naked, and they felt no shame (Genesis 2:18–25).

God created human beings as sexual beings. That's a plain and simple fact. But from the beginning, God put sexuality in the context of relationship. When God created Eve as companion for Adam, God said, "For this reason a man will leave his father and mother and be united to his wife, and they will become one flesh" (Genesis 2:24). Husband and wife promise themselves to each other and take responsibility for caring for each other. In the intimate commitment of sex, they become "one flesh." Sex is not merely physical. It is primarily relational. God created it for the marriage relationship.

God makes four points here, and he reaffirms them all throughout Scripture. Marriage is intended to be:

Monogamous: One man and one woman. From the beginning this was the plan as designed by God. He saw that it was good. Elsewhere in Scripture we see men taking multiple wives, surprisingly even David and Solomon. But just because Scripture records this, it does not mean God approved of it. These relationships were far from being God's ideal. His divine design for marriage is one man and one woman.

Heterosexual: The first relationship was designed to complete, to balance and to satisfy. Together they have the power to create life. Scripture is clear. There are no references to homosexual behavior or homosexual marriages that can be interpreted as having the approval of God. His plan has been and always will be for a "husband and wife."

Separate and Permanent: The first couple is specially designed for each other and they will be together throughout the rest of their story recorded in those early chapters of Genesis. Through the hardship of their sin and its consequences, and past the pain of a murdered son they stay together. They are together "till death parts them." They didn't have to take vows to understand the truth about their relationship. Together forever! This is the divine design.

Intimate: The two became one flesh and they were not ashamed. Sex is good and natural in the context of marriage. In the world before Adam and Eve's sin of disobeying God, guilt and shame did not exist. What a wonderful idea; unbridled intimacy!

Now let's look at a passage from the New Testament.

Wives, submit to your husbands as to the Lord. For the husband is the head of the wife as Christ is the head of the church, his body, of which he is the Savior. Now as the church submits to Christ, so also wives should submit to their husbands in everything.

Husbands, love your wives, just as Christ loved the church and gave himself up for her to make her holy, cleansing her by the washing with water through the word, and to present her to himself as a radiant church, without stain or wrinkle or any other blemish, but holy and blameless. In this same way, husbands ought to love their wives as their own bodies. He who loves his wife loves himself. After all, no one ever hated his own body, but he feeds and cares for it, just as Christ does the church—for we are members of his body. "For this reason a man will leave his father and mother and be united to his wife, and the two will become one flesh."

This is a profound mystery—but I am talking about Christ and the church. However, each one of you also must love his wife as he loves himself, and the wife must respect her husband (Ephesians 5:22–33).

This passage focuses specifically on the relationship between Christ and the Church and how it compares to the relationship between husbands and wives. The marriage covenant relationship draws us to another divine relationship, that between Jesus and his bride, the Church. When we tamper with the institution of marriage, we tamper with the only living word picture that describes God's love and his relationship to the Church. Four aspects of Christ's relationship with the Church speak to general principles of marriage.

The unity of Christ and the Church: Unity is important to God. Jesus prays for the unity of the Church shortly before his arrest (John 17). Jesus and the Father are One. And it is his desire in that same prayer that we in the Body of Christ would be unified. In marriage we are unified in "one flesh." And as the ceremony goes, "What God has joined together, let no one put asunder." Marriage is about unity; it is designed to be permanent, as permanent as Jesus' love for his bride, the Church.

The sacrificial love of Christ for the Church: The hallmark of marriage is love, honor and sacrifice.

I have had many counseling relationships with concerns about marriage. I usually like to have some special time with the husband alone to see what his expectations are and to see if any lies have crept  **into his understanding of his role in marriage. When I tell husbands in struggling marriages that they are to die for their wives, that their purpose is to serve their brides and to do everything in their power to participate in the presentation of their brides as complete and unblemished, they tend to be defensive and dumbfounded. This is not what they signed up for. And this is not how husbands in struggling marriages treat their brides.**

Husbands are the human representation of God's love for his Church. This means that the husband's will and dreams are not the most important aspect of the marriage. Loving his bride is the most important. Just as Christ gave up all authority and power to sacrifice himself for his bride, husbands must be prepared to die, in all ways, for the honor and restoration of their wives.

This is a challenging new thought for most husbands!

The headship of Christ over the Church, and the submission of the Church to him: Just as sacrificial love is difficult for men, submitting to husbands is difficult for many wives. They resist the idea on principle. If one person is submissive to another, then that must mean that they are not equal. In our western culture the concepts of equality and roles have been blurred. The creation story makes clear that God designed men and women to equally reflect the image of God. Obvious, too, in that story is that God designed their roles to be different. Just as Jesus and the Spirit submit to the Father though they are equal, the wife submits to the husband and yet is equal. It is again part of the living word picture of God and his love and plan for the Church.

Do you think most people marry with a foundational understanding of their roles in marriage? Why not?

Would it make a difference later if you knew this going into the marriage?

The delighting of the husband in his wife and the delighting of the wife in her husband: This idea is implied in this Ephesians passage but blatant in others. Remember the command that God gives the Israelites in Deuteronomy:

If a man has recently married, he must not be sent to war or have any other duty laid on him. For one year he is to be free to stay at home and bring happiness to the wife he has married (Deuteronomy 24:5).

Bring happiness to his wife! God is talking about more than just washing the windows and buying her candy! This delight of the Creator includes a positive view of sexuality:

Let your fountain be blessed, and rejoice in the wife of your youth, a lovely deer, and a graceful deer—may her breasts satisfy you always, may you ever be captivated by her love (Proverbs 5:18, 19).

In fact, husbands are *commanded* to delight physically in their wives, to be carried away with their love. The sexual relationship between husband and wife is one of abandonment to the other. This idea carries over to the New Testament:

The wife's body does not belong to her alone, but also to her husband. In the same way, the husband's body does not belong to him alone but also to his wife (1 Corinthians 7:4).

Our bodies belong to each other, and are to be used within the marriage relationship to bind us together, and to give great pleasure to the other. So erotic love is not only sanctioned by the Bible, but also *commanded* within the confines of marriage. And all to the glory of God!

This is the ideal, and every marriage falls short. We make mistakes in every phase of our lives, and marriage is no exception. God desires for us to enjoy the fullness of marriage, and whatever our mistakes in marriage, we can start today to draw close to the ideal of Christian marriage by depending on the power of God. As we gain a deeper understanding of God's ideal for marriage, many of us will see the stark contrast with our own marriages. Satan will try to use that contrast to make you think, "This is hopeless. I am a failure as a husband or wife. My marriage can never reflect this ideal." God commands us not to be discouraged or afraid, because he himself is with us (Deuteronomy 31:8).

SEX OUTSIDE OF MARRIAGE

God designed sex for marriage, and only for married partners. Scripture calls sex outside of marriage fornication and sex with someone other

When we tamper with the institution of marriage,

we tamper with the only living word picture that describes

God's love and his relationship to the Church.

than your spouse adultery. This behavior is condemned as unholy, unrighteous, impure and immoral. Here are some verses that may help when you talk with your teen about this subject.

You shall not commit adultery (Exodus 10:14).

For out of the heart come evil thoughts, murder, adultery, sexual immorality, theft, false testimony, slander (Matthew 15:19).

Do you not know that your bodies are members of Christ himself? Shall I then take the members of Christ and unite them with a prostitute? Never! Do you not know that he who unites himself with a prostitute is one with her in body? For it is said, 'The two will become one flesh.' But he who unites himself with the Lord is one with him in spirit. Flee from sexual immorality. All other sins a man commits are outside his body, but he who sins sexually sins against his own body. Do you not know that your body is a temple of the Holy Spirit, who is in you, whom you have received from God? You are not your own; you were bought at a price. Therefore honor God with your body (1 Corinthians 6:15–20).

MODELING, THE BEST KIND OF TALK

Kids watch their parents closely. Very young children watch and imitate as part of their normal development. Older kids and teens have learned habits and attitudes that may stay with them the rest of their lives. And most teenagers have acquired some pretty good debating skills, so they can logically refute a lot of what you say. They may even use your own behaviors as evidence that you don't believe what you say. Ouch!

Married couples have an awesome opportunity to be a picture of self-sacrificial love to their kids. Many parents would say they sacrifice their whole lives for their kids, and it certainly seems that way at times. After a baby is born, we have to wait about 20 years before we can do

Marriage is not just a social convention.

It's not merely a legal status. It's God's idea!

something for ourselves instead of always tending to the needs of children! We hope that someday our kids will recognize what we've done for them. But every day, as parents interact with each other, they paint a picture of how to be married.

Thoughtfulness.

Consideration.

Self-sacrifice.

Partnership.

Affectionate touches.

Do your kids see these things in the way you relate to your spouse? Do they see a relational context for sexuality?

Some of you are saying, "But I'm not married any more. And the relationship was so bad that it was no way to teach kids about marriage." You have a unique opportunity to teach your kids what it is to know forgiveness.

If we confess our sins, he is faithful and just and will forgive us our sins and purify us from all unrighteousness (1 John 1:9).

Have you received God's forgiveness for the failures that led to divorce? Or have you extended forgiveness to a former spouse? What are you modeling to your kids even in a less-than-ideal situation?

Whether you are married or single at this point in your life, take a few minutes to reflect on what you'd like your kids to understand about marriage.

When I got married, I thought marriage was…

Now I know that marriage is…

**The most important thing I want my son or daughter
to understand about marriage is…**

The verse that helps me understand marriage the most is…

I can help my child understand God's idea of marriage by…

Marriage is not just a social convention. It's not merely a legal status. It's God's idea! He created marriage as the perfect context for his gift of sexuality. That's what kids need to know!

quesTIons anD Answers

You would think that in this age of information, finding a good answer to a difficult question would be easy. It would be, except for one simple flaw in the system. More is not necessarily better.

Today's post-modern cultural philosophy puts Truth and Knowledge on the endangered species list. The philosophies of relativism (no absolute moral truths) and pluralism (every idea is equally valid) are rapidly gaining acceptance in our educational system as well as popular culture. Those who cling to the idea of absolute truth are labeled as intolerant, bigoted and narrow-minded. Christianity is often considered out of step with society and too narrow to be relevant in today's culture.

These post-modern ideas are killing our teens. Every idea is not equal, and untruths can kill. Teens need direction, so they need direct answers. They especially need direct answers to their questions about sexuality, intimacy and love. Your kids have questions—but you have questions, too. "What do I need to say?" "How do I get started?" "What if...?" "How about...?" It's okay to have questions. It's okay to admit that you don't feel fully prepared to talk to your kids about sexuality. You'll have new questions months or years from now as your kids, especially teenagers, face situations you've haven't thought of yet.

In the following pages you will find questions and answers about how to talk to your kids about sexuality. Some of them are based in fact and statistics. Others are suggestions for how you might handle a particular situation. You may or may not agree with the responses, but you cannot ride the fence anymore. It is time to have an opinion, one based on solid fact, sound wisdom and biblical truth. And it is time to share it with your kids.

One evening at the conclusion of one of my teen Lamaze classes I decided to ask Rebecca a question. I had just taught contraception, which I did in those days, as the girls had all been sexually active (I'm not sure I'd make that same choice today, but I was young at that time). I asked Rebecca why  she was in the class again. This was Rebecca's third baby and she was barely 17 years old. The first two babies she had aborted and this one she was going to deliver and parent.

I asked, "Rebecca, you know this stuff (contraception information) better than I do. Why are you here again? How is it that you are pregnant again when you know how to use all of this?"

Rebecca answered, "I have a rule." She was then silent, so I decided to press my luck.

"A rule?" I asked. "What sort of rule?"

"If I'm in a date's apartment or bedroom for more than a half-hour then I have to do it."

"Do you mean have sex?" I asked in shock.

"Ya," Rebecca answered. "That's just the way it is. I owe it."

I left the hospital that night about midnight still shaken. It was the beginning of the Lord putting the light bulb on for me. I started to realize that information and knowledge alone mean nothing because the "rules" out in the world overcome all of the excellent information. If the truth is not spoken in love, kids will believe all kinds of lies. It's only truth in relationship that changes lives.

How do I begin this talk when it's really embarrassing!

Most parents don't talk to their teens about sex because it's too embarrassing. Many feel disqualified to talk to their teens about sex and abstinence because they were not abstinent before marriage. It is difficult when we have made choices ourselves as teens that we now consider wrong for our own children. But this doesn't mean that we don't have to talk with our teens about God's truth and good choices. In fact, it makes it even more important to talk with them. Teens need to make the right choices. Their lives depend on it.

Don't feel that you have to press the subject of sex all the time. Use a teachable moment, such as during a TV show. Calmly and briefly point out the lies that are communicated in the show. Do the same with magazines or other forms of media that your kids use. Sex is a very personal subject. Talking about it in a brief but timely manner is a good way to make sure that teens know your values and a biblical viewpoint on the subject.

What do I do if I find condoms in my teen's bedroom?

First of all, don't panic. Talk the situation over with your spouse, trusted friend or pastor. Decide how best to approach your son or daughter. Waiting for a day or so for your emotions to cool down is often a good idea.

Talk to your teen in privacy with your spouse. Never confront your teen in front of siblings or guests in your home. Treat your teen with dignity and love, but confront directly. Ask direct questions. "Are you having sex?" "How long have you been having sex?" Ask if your daughter or your son's girlfriend has had a pregnancy test. Ask if they have been checked for STDs. Then take whatever action you and your spouse believe is appropriate for your family.

Remember, many teens are relieved when their parents discover their sexual activity. Many times they do not want to be sexually active and are caught in coerced into having sex. Initially you may have an angry teen on your hands but, in time, the young person will experience great relief to be out of the cycle of guilt, shame and lies.

Does signing a purity pledge card have any effect on my teen's behavior?

Yes, research shows that signing a pledge card may decrease the chances of a teen having sex outside of marriage. But keeping a teen pure takes much more than a pledge card. People are often influenced in their decisions by relationships. Teens need their parents and other adult mentors to walk each day with them. They need mentors with the character of Christ to teach them and to answer questions. Mentors need to be present in the teen's life and accessible when the teen needs advice or just needs to talk.

How do I talk about the consequences today of premarital sex?

Prepare for this discussion by thinking about the changes since you were young. Some of the consequences of premarital sex are the same as when we parents were teenagers. People still get broken hearts (emotional consequences). People who have had one or more partners may think about previous partners even when they want to be faithful to their spouse (mental consequences). Teens are still getting pregnant. And there is still separation from God because of sin (spiritual consequences). However, some physical consequences are very different from the 1960s. At that time there were only two sexually transmitted diseases (STDs). Today there are more than 25 STDs. People will suffer lifelong consequences from some of these diseases because there is no cure. Be ready with solid information and facts to share with your teen. He or she may not know all the information necessary to make good choices. Chapters 10 and 11 will give you more information about the consequences of premarital sex.

How can I help my child who has been exposed to pornography?

There are at least three things to keep in mind when children are exposed to pornography.

As with all bad choices our children make, the goal is to restore them to health and for them to experience God's forgiveness. For many parents the issue of pornography is particularly difficult to deal with confidently and lovingly. Avoid angry and shaming statements. Instead, confront with the motivation to correct and restore.

All of us need person-centered boundaries and accountability to help us with temptations. Every child is different, depending on age and personality. Put screening software on your computer and limit Internet use to when you are home. Keep tabs on friends and what may be available at other homes. Communicate clear consequences for future failings and consistently enforce them. Kids who are old enough to hide pornography are also old enough to know the risks and downsides.

Education is important, but education alone won't keep children away from risky behaviors. Talk about honoring God and our bodies all the time. Model making great choices yourself and be forgiving in your home all of the time, not just when a bad choice is discovered.

Chapter 9 on Hot Topics has more information about pornography and its effect on kids.

How do we (I) determine consequences for unacceptable behavior?

An important aspect of any punishment is that the consequences are known ahead of time and that they fit the "crime." Establish ground rules with your children, either individually or in a family meeting during their preteen years. Talk about boundaries in dating, curfew, drug and alcohol use and any other important topic. Be clear what the punishment will be when rules are broken and always follow through with the predetermined consequences. Rules and consequences give a teen a measure of safety and clearly communicate caring on the part of the parents.

Is there a fun way to demonstrate or talk about boundaries?

One way to talk about boundaries is an activity called the "hot seat." One family or several families can talk about boundaries this game format. Arrange several chairs in front of the group, leaving one chair empty. Ask for several volunteers to be the "experts." The experts sit in the chairs in the front, except for the extra chair that remains empty. One person in the audience asks a question about relationships, sex, boundaries, curfews, dating, etc. and the experts give their answers. If someone from the audience wants to answer he or she must come up and temporarily fill the empty chair, give an answer and return to his or her seat. This is a comfortable way for parents and teens to share and listen to other opinions regarding a given subject.

How does a parent regain trust in a child who has ignored rules and violated boundaries?

Trust is always earned and love is always given. This is an important truth, whether you are a parent or a teenager. If trust is lost it takes a long time of trustworthy behavior to regain it. The restoration of trust is determined by the person who feels the distrust, not by the person who has broken the trust.

Can sexually transmitted diseases lead to infertility problems?

According to the American Society of Reproductive Medicine infertility has several major causes. Conception depends upon many factors including: 1) the production of healthy sperm and healthy eggs; 2) unblocked fallopian tubes that allow the sperm to reach the egg (STDs can cause the tubes to become blocked); 3) the sperm's ability to fertilize the egg; 4) the ability of the fertilized egg to become implanted in the woman's uterus and; 5) sufficient quality of the newly formed life. The malfunction of any of these systems can potentially cause infertility. Female teens are more susceptible to STD infections for several reasons, including the immaturity of the reproductive system. And with some STD infections females have no symptoms (asymptomatic), so they can experience significant destruction of their fallopian tubes before they know they are infected with a disease. Because of this asymptomatic nature of some of the most common STDs, that sexually active teens should be screened for STDs every six months. Remember, diseases can be spread by many sexual practices besides vaginal intercourse. Chapter 10 has more information about STDs.

Are any STDs transmitted through the use of public bathrooms?

Most STDs are very fragile and die easily outside of the body. The air often dries these germs quickly and they soon die. Studies of some STDs, however, show that they can stay alive longer in warm, moist environments outside of the body such as on the surfaces of hot tubs. It is always a good practice not to sit on an uncovered toilet seat;

although a person may not contract an STD, he or she may contract other pathogens.

How do we convince teens that oral sex is sex?

Be direct about what you think. It is important when talking with our preteens and teens that they understand that all sexual activity is sex. Whether people are actively engaging in vaginal intercourse, anal intercourse, oral sex or mutual masturbation, it is all considered sex. Any of these types of sexual practices are capable of spreading STDs. It is all considered sex in God's eyes. Listen for the ways the word "sex" is used in conversations or reading material that your teen hears or sees. Use that as a springboard for conversation. If our bodies are truly God's temple then we should always honor him in the way that we use them. And Scripture is clear that sex is a gift that God has given us for marriage.

How do I begin a discussion of abstinence if teens are already sexually active?

A common misconception of Christian parents and leaders is that teens who go to church or youth group are not sexually active. There is no statistical difference between Christian and non-Christian teens when it comes to sexual activity. It is more common, however, to hear Christian teens practicing alternative forms of sex rather than vaginal penetration. They are interested in being technical virgins for marriage. It is important for teens to focus on honoring God rather than on being technical virgins. If their activities are not honoring God, then they need to stop, ask for forgiveness and move to honoring activities.

Whenever a group discussion occurs with teens, assume that some are or have been sexually active. Along with healthy choices and spiritual truth, it's important to talk about God's forgiveness and grace. Secondary virginity is a concept that allows for a teen who was sexually active to begin again. He or she cannot regain virginity but can make a decision to remain abstinent from now until the day of marriage. This is a new beginning and a way to now honor a future husband or wife.

What kind of information impacts teens the most? Statistics? Emotional consequences? Fear and Guilt?

It is always important to tell your teenagers the truth about diseases, teen pregnancy and all of the consequences of sexual behaviors. Teenagers tend to pay attention to true stories more than raw statistics. They can relate to stories about other teens and the consequences that they suffered due to poor choices. So communicating the truth, whether through statistics or stories, works well with most teens. Parents know what learning style works best with their child. Use that style no matter what you are teaching them and it will be most effective for that individual.

What should I say when my child asks about my first time?

Many parents of today's teens have the distinction of being part of the "free love" generation because they were teenagers in the 1960s and 1970s. Many parents did not save sex until marriage. If you were sexually active before marriage, it is your decision as to whether or not to tell your teen. It is one of the most personal parts of your history and it is not necessary to share it.

A few cautions if you are in the midst of this decision. Once you have shared this with a teen he or she can use it as a weapon against you. Discern very carefully if this is a young adult who can handle this information without bringing back the inconsistencies to you every time you set a rule or guideline. Secondly, share all of the consequences of this behavior. Your teen needs to know the physical, mental, emotional and spiritual consequences of your action. Otherwise, it will seem to your child that there were no consequences for you and, therefore, no consequences for him or her.

Remember, you are forgiven for your past mistakes through Jesus Christ. Every good thing designed by God can be destroyed and perverted. That includes the gift of sexual intimacy. This is the result of sin. God has shown his great love for us by providing his Son as a payment or ransom for our sin, even the sin of sexual immorality. In his Son, we can be holy and righteous, regardless of our past.

For if you forgive men when they sin against you, your heavenly Father will also forgive you. But if you do not forgive men their sins, your Father will not forgive your sins (Matthew 6:14, 15).

And when you stand praying, if you hold anything against anyone, forgive him, so that your Father in heaven may forgive you your sins. (Mark 11:25).

If we confess our sins, he is faithful and just and will forgive us our sins and purify us from all unrighteousness (1 John 1:9).

This is love: not that we loved God, but that he loved us and sent his Son as an atoning sacrifice for our sins (1 John 4:10).

Forget the former things; do not dwell on the past. See, I am doing a new thing! Now it springs up; do you not perceive it? I am making a way in the desert and stream in the wasteland (Isaiah 43:18, 19).

HELP FOR TOUGH QUESTIONS

Getting help to answer the tough questions your teens may ask about sex is a great idea. Getting good help is even a better idea. These days many people sit down at the computer and start clicking for answers. Here are some important tips that will help you wade through the web.

- **Make sure you are in the right place.**
  Does this site address the topic you are researching? Is the URL address correct?

- **When in doubt, there is probably good reason.**
  Do you have good reason to believe that the information on the site *is accurate?* Is there supporting evidence for the material being presented?

- **Consider the source.**
  Does the sponsor of the website have a political or philosophical bias that may influence the reporting of information?
  Is this a commercial, governmental, personal or academic website?

• **Know what's "being sold."**

What is the purpose of the site? Is the main purpose to inform, to persuade, or to sell you something? Do you understand what is being said or left unsaid?

And when it is all said and done, always double check your information against the truth of Scripture. If the information you have been given goes against the spiritual laws and moral absolutes of God, then it doesn't matter how many research articles support it. Our children are too important to trust to a quick look on the web. Better to study Scripture, seek wise counsel, pray without ceasing and walk by faith not by sight!

We demolish arguments and every pretension that sets itself up against the knowledge of God, and we take captive every thought to make it obedient to Christ (2 Corinthians 10:5).

THE PRIME DIRECTIVE

Do you remember the "Prime Directive"? It is a value statement that serves as the ultimate non-negotiable of space travel as we know it from the TV series *Star Trek*. If you are not a "Trekkie," you may not be aware that Star Trek was so philosophical. Here is the Prime Directive as stated on the series:

As the right of each sentient species to live in accordance with its normal cultural evolution is considered sacred, no Star Fleet personnel may interfere with the healthy development of alien life and culture. Such interference includes the introduction of superior knowledge, strength or technology to a world whose society is incapable of handling such advantages wisely. Star Fleet personnel may not violate this Prime Directive, even to save their lives and/or their ship unless they are acting to right an earlier violation or an accidental contamination of said culture. This directive takes precedence over any and all other considerations, and carries with it the highest moral obligation.

What Star Fleet command said in its strongest terms is that under penalty of death, no space traveler can mess with the culture of another space species, not even to stay alive. It is the most sacred of ideas. Every species' belief and culture is to be unchallenged. This is a profound worldview and it is absolutely contrary to the Christian worldview.

When *Star Trek*, the original series, first aired, Baby Boomers were teens! *Star Trek: The Next Generation* first aired in 1987. Today's teens have never known anything but *Star Trek* and the Prime Directive.

The best lie is the subtle lie. Slowly sneak it in through casual conversation, a dropped hint, an inconsequential TV show. The not-so-subtle conclusion that has shaped our entire "Next Generation" of young people is that no one has the market on Truth. No one has the right to tell another person what to do, what is important and what to believe.

We live in a world of lies, and the lie being spread here is that God is not Truth. He is not the Life. He is not necessarily the Way. Maybe one way, but not *the* one way. Teens and college students hear this over and over and over. They cannot escape this subtle lie. It is in their music, their classrooms and, double check, maybe in your home or church youth group. If you believe this lie, then you can believe the lie that anyone mature enough to have sex physically and emotionally can and should enjoy it, and that sex is a personal thing between two people and how they enjoy that is of no concern to anyone else. Sound familiar?

Friends, believing this is not freedom; it's slavery. Helping your kids

Spell Check

In September 2003, federal agents arrested a man who allegedly was running a website to direct children to graphic sex sites. He used addresses that children might use to look for Disneyland or Teletubbies, simply switching or omitting letters in the legitimate addresses. A child who transposed letters or misspelled a site address might end up in a pornographic site instead of Disneyland. Then the child would encounter a maze of pop-up advertising that brought up even more ads when the user tried to back out of the site or close windows.

A section of the Truth in Domain Names law makes it a crime to use a misleading domain name with the intent to deceive a minor into viewing material that is harmful.

The Internet is full of ways to lie, cheat and steal that didn't exist 25 years ago.

understand God's plan for sexuality and the beauty and mystery of marriage is a far greater gift. So ask the questions you need to ask to get ready for this task. Talk with trusted friends and research the tough topics. Encourage your children to ask all the questions they want to ask in a safe, trusting environment—your home. If they ask something you don't know the answer to, find the answer together. Above all, walk boldly in the truth.

DO YOU TRUST THE INTERNET?

In a national poll commissioned by Streaming Media, 1,232 respondents were asked about what sources they trust the most for news. Of the 550 regular Internet users in the poll, 76% said they could learn everything they need to know from the net; 51% said the Internet had the most accurate information. *(Source: Editor and Publisher, May 15, 2000.)*

In a Pew Internet Survey on education and the Internet, 71% of online teens say that they used the Internet as the major source for their most recent major school project or report.

In a Pew Internet Survey on health and the internet, 52 million American adults, or 55% of those with Internet access, have used the web to get health or medical information. Many say the resources they find on the web have a direct effect on the decisions they make about their health care and interaction with doctors. Ten percent have purchased medicine or vitamins online.

Getting your sex education on the Internet is more than dangerous. Even sites that you would assume to be trustworthy have been accused of purposely withholding information, distorting information and bold-faced deception. The Internet is definitely a wealth of information, but it is not all true.

chapter eight

INTIMACY AND Boundaries

I didn't attend Sunday school much when I was growing up. So when I got the chance to take my daughters when they were young, I liked

to tag along! They did such fun things; color, cut out things, paste things, eat the paste; things like that. And of course they would sing. I love to sing and I was impressed by the theology in these simple children's songs. Take for instance this classic:

Be careful little eyes, what you see.
Be careful little eyes, what you see.
There's a Father up above, looking down in tender love,
So be careful little eyes, what you see.

And not content to let that first great verse be the end, the song goes on to make a series of "Reality Statements." Verse two encourages little ears to be careful what they hear, verse three warns little mouths what they might say, verse four cautions little hands to be careful what they touch and the final verse admonishes little feet to be careful where they go.

Psychologists tell us that every image, smell and sound we experience is filed somewhere in the remarkable human brain. Those of us who have moved away from our childhood homes and returned for a visit know how true this is. Certain sights, sounds and smells that have long since faded from our awareness come back to us. Memories we didn't know we had rush over us. Our emotions swirl with the surfacing thoughts. It's real. Let's unpack our little song with this in mind.

"Be careful!"

The first good theology lesson not so hidden in this lyric is that we have a huge responsibility. The secret to mental, physical, social and spiritual health is...careful choices. Duh! And apparently we have to make them for ourselves. No one can make them for us. And there is no one to blame but ourselves. God says we can have wisdom and truth if we only ask. So ask!

"Eyes, ears, mouth, hands and feet."

What is that all about? The song describes two ways to learn: watch and listen. And then it describes three ways to respond: what we say, what we do and where we go. In a world saturated with sexual images and innuendo, this is terrific advice. We have to be very careful what our eyes see and our ears hear. These are the doorways to our hearts and minds.

"There is a Father up above looking down in tender love."

Finally, and perhaps the most important: the Motive! This is not a cosmic guilt trip, like some of us are afraid of. God is a loving Father, not a policeman. Watching in love, not judgment. He wants the best for us, and the "great cloud of witnesses" we read about in Hebrews 11 is cheering for us, not watching for mistakes. This is really Good News!

When it comes to sexual sin, having great boundaries about what we let into our mind is critical. X-rated images from the movie screen, explicit lyrics from a haunting rap never go away. They just sink below our awareness, until sometime in the future, a sight or sound dredges them up. Our Lord Jesus strongly challenges his disciples to have eyes to see and ears to hear, but the implication is to have eyes and ears for the truth alone.

But understanding how we take in information is only half the trick. We have to respond to this truth with how we behave. James encourages us to not just listen to the Word, but do what it says (James 1:22). James goes on to note that all too often, "The tongue is also a fire, a world of evil among the parts of the body. It corrupts the whole person, sets the whole course of his life on fire" (James 3:6). Lies are like poison, so we truly do have to watch what we say. We have to watch where we go. Jesus said over and over "Follow me!" He wants us to put our thumbs in his spiritual belt loops and hang on, stepping in his footprints. If we walk where he walks and step where he steps, our little feet will be safe!

UNDERSTANDING INTIMACY

Intimacy. What a great idea. Everybody wants it, yet everyone is afraid of it! What in the world does it mean anymore? In a sex-saturated culture like ours intimacy and sex have become synonymous. But somewhere in the front of our minds, we know that intimacy is something powerful and elusive. Teens force the issue, married couples

> **Our goal as parents is to teach our teenagers
> to find intimacy and at the same time control their
> sexual desires and behaviors.**

dance in and out of intimacy and disciples long to be intimate with their God. Our goal as parents is to teach our teenagers to find intimacy and at the same time control their sexual desires and behavior. No small effort! We are going to have to help them understand what intimacy is and what it isn't, and what happens when intimacy goes bad.

Let's start with what *isn't* intimacy.

It isn't just sex, though sex certainly is an intimate act. When asked for the definition of intimacy, the first thought for many of us is sexual. But an "intimate act" is not the same thing as "intimacy." In Denmark, where hardcore sex is sold openly on the streets and pornographic TV is just one more channel on cable, sex is reduced to biology. There is no intimacy whatsoever in the most intimate of acts.

What a sadness it must be for God to see sex used so casually. Designed by God to help bond a marriage, sex outside of the power and purpose of marriage is like pulling the engine out of a car and firing it up. You can do it, it may even be fun, but it won't ever take you anywhere!

It isn't familiarity, though in an intimate relationship, we would most likely know the person very well. It is not unusual to be familiar with someone and not to be intimate. You may be the same age, have many similar past and present experiences, live in the same culture, have children the same age and still not be intimate with your friend.

It isn't just shared experiences, though this, too, would be expected in an intimate friendship. Shared experiences are important to building friendships, but you may have lots of people that you regularly do things with, but you have never really opened up and learned about the deepest parts of who you are. Most of us are not intimate, just busy!

It is not marriage. Getting married is no more a guarantee for intimacy than expecting to become an expert in mathematics just by declaring a math major. It is a good start, but intimacy in marriage is a long-term effort. The longer the true goal of intimacy stays alive in marriage, the better chance there is for intimacy to "break out." Too many marriage counselors have seen couples married many years who are still not intimate. What a tragedy!

> **Why do you think so many people never experience**
> **true intimacy? Do you think people are afraid of love? How so?**

Some sociologists believe that intimacy has been bleached out of our culture in the pursuit of comfort, money, positions of influence and prestige. We don't have a lot of good models to go by.

God designed us to be intimate with him. To be fully known and to be fully enjoyed forever! The Bible suggests that the spiritual key to a healthy sexual life is *intimacy*. The second and third chapters of Genesis describe the meaning of our sexual selves in the great story of Adam and Eve. Adam says of Eve, "This is now bone of my bone and flesh of my flesh." The next verse says, "a man will leave his father and mother and be united to his wife, and they will become one flesh" (Genesis 2:24). This is a deep and powerful union of souls. Then, in Genesis 4:1, "Adam lay with his wife Eve, and she became pregnant and gave birth to Cain."

But something went all wrong—*sin*. Now we, as descendents of Adam and Eve, search for intimacy in all the wrong places. In some ways it is a miracle that young people control their sexual desires at all, given the fact that sexual images and temptation are everywhere and there are so few models of true intimacy.

True intimacy is about being known fully as a whole person. It includes all the aspects of our lives. The physical (and that *might* include sex), but also the mental, social, emotional and spiritual aspects of us. Intimacy involves risk, transparency and overcoming the fear of being exposed; being seen for who you really are. Intimacy comes to the point where it asks the question, "Here I am completely open and exposed, blemishes and scars, the good and the bad. Will you still love me?" What a moment of fear that is!

Marshall Hodge wrote a book called *Your Fear of Love*. In it he says, "We long for moments of expressions of love, closeness and tenderness, but frequently, at the critical point, we often draw back. We are afraid of closeness. We are afraid of love." Later in the same book Hodge states, "The closer you come to somebody, the greater potential there is for pain." This fear of rejection and pain often drives us away from finding true intimacy.

Let's look at these aspects of who we are more closely.

Social intimacy asks the question, "Do I know your friends and family? Do I know why you love them or don't love them? What they enjoy in you and what you enjoy about them?" Making social intimacy an important value tells your partner you care abut the other important people in his or her life, the people that influenced and shaped this life you so want to know.

Mental intimacy sounds funny, but the idea is the ideas. "What do you believe in and why? What is important to you, what are your highest values, the non-negotiables in your life? What are your dreams, what do you want to be when you grow up?" When I know what is in your head, what preoccupies your mind, I know you so much more. When I share with you an unrealized dream, you may love me and believe in me enough to help me reach it. This is intimacy!

Emotional Intimacy. For about half of us this makes sense. Women seem to understand the emotional side of relationships better than most men. Identifying with another's feelings goes a long way toward establishing intimacy. "What are your feelings and how intense are they? Do they come out of an event in your past or some recent experience? Do these feelings overwhelm you or have you been pushing them down to protect yourself?" Scripture says there is a time to weep and a time to laugh (Ecclesiastes 3:4). Connecting emotionally builds intimacy.

Physical intimacy seems obvious, and in many ways it is. The more sexually intimate we become with a person, the more we know them. In fact, the Old Testament term for sex was "to know." But there are other ways to build intimacy on the physical side. Being on a sports team, learning to work on a hobby together, working alongside someone, all these are physical aspects of who we are that can build intimacy without crossing the boundaries of sexual behavior. And having sex with someone doesn't necessarily build intimacy.

Spiritual intimacy is sharing the deepest most vital part of who you are. Your personality, your essence. It is the most intimate part of you, as it is the truest part of you. But it is also the most mysterious past. You may not even know your own inner spirit at all. And if that is true, how can you hope to share it with someone else? Our culture is just now becoming "spiritually" popular again. People are buying prayer beads, dolphin pins, crystal chimes and dream catchers, all expressions of an increase in attending to the spiritual part of who we are.

Which kind of intimacy do you find the most challenging to achieve? Why do you think that is?

God wants to have an intimate walk with his people. Our sin separates us from him and every relationship suffers. The great news is that we have a Savior who has ransomed us from this fate!

This truth about our whole person has a huge impact on our relationships. If we emphasize one aspect of who we are, put all of our time into that one dynamic, the other parts of who we are go unexplored. If the area focused on is the sexual side of physical intimacy, it can be so powerful and consuming that the relationship becomes a sham.

In this kind of relationship, intimacy is out of control, out of balance, and the relationship has almost no chance of maturing. Too often teens view the dating relationship in high school almost like a marriage. Relationships are exclusive and intimate, but without the committed protection of the marriage covenant. When the relationship

Some sociologists believe that intimacy has been bleached out of our culture.

We don't have a lot of good models to go by.

breaks off, as most do, it as though this 14-, 15-, 16-year-old couple is going through a divorce. Each time they date, get intimate and break up, a part of their self-worth is destroyed. Perhaps worse, it begins the habit of believing that "relationships don't last" and this lie slips into a future marriage relationship. The popular impression that Hollywood has reinforced is that marriages can come and go, and when it gets tough it's okay to call it off. Marriage vows are increasingly being rewritten to be less constraining.

Within marriage the powerful experience of sex can build trust and commitment and can be nurtured so that the ever-present fear of abandonment can be calmed. I can be fully and honestly "me." In healthy young adult or teen dating relationships, God has directed us to build intimacy first in other ways and to save the physical act of sexual intimacy for marriage. Physical intimacy is confined to wholesome activities like playing Frisbee, teaching the dog to fetch, learning to play guitar together or other kinds of physical activity that build intimacy without sex.

For a young person to achieve intimacy is very rare. It is hard enough for those of us who are older and in a marriage relationship. Harriet Learner in *The Dance of Intimacy* discusses the delicate dance between the "us" and "me." On the one hand we need to connect better with ourselves and set good personal boundaries. On the other, we need to loosen our preoccupation with ourselves, learn to be more other-centered and be genuinely present with the other person. If we go too far out of ourselves toward our partner, we start to lose ourselves. And yet if we hold back and remain too self-contained, no deep contact is possible. Learner suggests that in a really intimate relationship each person shares, sacrifices, and is true to himself or herself, and each party expresses strength and vulnerability, weakness and competence in a balanced way.

It is tricky. Many counseling clients have been hurt in love and vow never to let that happen again.

I was giving a series of talks at a family camp in the Puget Sound of Washington. After one of the meetings, a teenage girl came up to me and said, "I have to talk to you about my boyfriend problems." We sat down, and she began telling me her troubles. After a few moments, she made this statement: "I am now taking steps never to get hurt again." I said to her, "In other words, you are taking steps never to love again." She had thought I misunderstood, so she continued. "No, that's not what I am saying. I just don't want to get hurt anymore. I don't want pain in my life." I said, "That's right, you don't want love in your life." You see, there is no such thing as "painless love." The closer we come to somebody, the greater potential there is for pain.

DAVE'S STORY

Most of us would say we have been hurt in a relationship before. If we are honest, all of us have. The question is, how do you handle that hurt? In order to camouflage the pain, a lot of us give confusing verbal and non-verbal messages. I flirt, wanting you to come close, but then when you do come close, I close off and push you away. We say to a person, "Look, I want you to come closer to me. I want to love and be loved...but wait a minute. I've been hurt before. No, I don't want to get this close. I don't want to feel these emotions." We build walls around our hearts to protect us from anyone on the outside getting in to hurt us. But that same wall that keeps people out keeps us stuck inside. The result? Loneliness sets in and true intimacy and love become impossible. As a parent or caring adult, it may be time to look deep inside our own hearts to see if God can heal us from the inside out.

So intimacy is a risk. A huge risk! I share a secret with you and you share one with me. If neither of us betrays the other, we might risk sharing another dream, failure, victory, temptation, frustration or regret. In an intimate relationship, you know me without the mask. But the gift is that if you still love me anyway, you love the true me, not a cardboard cut-out that I have been showing off. Now I am free to love and be loved in truth!

Who besides God knows you the best?
How did this person get to know you so well?

UNDERSTANDING AND CONTROLLING SEXUAL DESIRES

Helping our youth control their sexual desires means first understanding the steps of intimacy and then using self-control to set great boundaries in terms of sexual behavior.

So how many steps of intimacy are there? John Trent identifies eight steps. Author Roberta Russell maintains that there are 22 steps to intimacy. Others say four or six. But no one seems to argue that there are no steps. Probably the best study was discussed by Oxford Zoologist Dr. Desmond Morris in his 1967 book, *The Naked Ape*, referring, of course, to humans. Using his observation skills, he identifies 12 steps of intimacy, a process that all people go through as they build romantic connections. He lists them as follows, each step representing more risk of exposure and increasingly deeper intimacy:

these stages represent a progression of physical intimacy
that moves from very modest to very intimate.

1
EYE
TO BODY

2
EYE
TO EYE

3
VOICE
TO VOICE

4
HAND
TO HAND

5
HAND TO
SHOULDER

6
HAND
TO WAIST

7
FRONT
TO FRONT

8
LIP
TO LIP

9
HAND
TO BREAST

10
MOUTH
TO BREAST

11
TOUCHING
BELOW
THE WAIST

12
INTERCOURSE

Understanding this process is critical to controlling sexual desires in the context of a relationship. It is important to remember that once a relationship has passed through one of the gates of intimacy, the next time you connect as a couple you will begin where you left off. In our fast-paced world that wants love and intimacy to be just as fast as our food and cars, speeding up the process of physical intimacy can be disastrous. We are tempted to skip some of these gates. In the movies they do it all the time. We hurry through each step, longing for the intimacy of the next, not counting the risks of skipping the process along the way.

The last four steps of this process are considered by most to be foreplay. Foreplay is defined by www.dictionary.com as "mutual sexual stimulation prior to sexual intercourse."

Really, it is a kind of a promise. When couples get to these steps in the intimacy process, they are in essence saying to each other, "I intend to satisfy you and I intend to be satisfied." Every aspect of who we are—physical, emotional and psychological—all are being prepared for sex. The acts of foreplay are not acts that can be mistaken for platonic love.

But that doesn't mean that holiness is preserved just by avoiding foreplay? So many teens just want the answer to the age-old question, "How far can I go?" When that question is asked, the goal is to see how close we can get to sin without actually sinning. This is the attitude of the Sadducees and Pharisees that Jesus became so enraged at, an attitude of shortsighted legalism rather than pure, unadulterated holiness. Jesus would rather have us ask the question, "Where do I need to stand to be in an unbridled, intimate relationship with God?" Many young people need to seriously consider setting their boundaries before the step of kissing. Kissing, especially French kissing, is an intimate act that, to most of us, communicates love and commitment.

One good idea is to set a "last ditch" boundary before the dating relationship even starts. Begin with the idea that any "touching where the swimsuit would touch" is off limits, and then add to that the rule that "if anything gets unbuttoned, unzipped, untucked or undone," it is time to get out of that setting! Fast!

Jeff came into my office for counseling. He was 16 years old at the time. He started off by saying, "I think I have a sexual addiction. I know I need help."

Looking at Jeff I saw an ordinary young man, from a great Christian home. He played soccer and the trumpet. He was a regular attendee at his church youth group, part of the youth worship team. He was clean-cut, good-looking, quiet-spoken.

DAVE'S STORY

Jeff led off. "Every time I start dating, the relationship turns sexual. I say to myself not this time, but it always happens.

I made a promise that I would date only Christian girls, but they seem to be as obsessed as I am." His head fell and his voice quieted.

"I got started with porn when I was 13. My friend had videos at his house that he had borrowed from his father's collection. I ended up taking some of them home and watching them over and over. I couldn't get the images out of my mind."

Jeff paused for a couple of minutes and gathered himself. "I never thought I would be in a situation like this. My girlfriend is pregnant. She is just 14. Our parents don't know yet. My girlfriend is their only child. It is going to be hell."

He looked back up at me and repeated over and over, "I'm not a bad guy. I am not a bad guy. What do I do? What do I do?"

If Jeff were your son, what would you say to him?

**What steps could Jeff's parents have taken
to help prevent this situation?**

All the good answers for Jeff are over. The easy choices are gone, but he can still make "right choices." Somewhere along the line he fell victim to two deadly lies.

The first lie was, "This is just between her and me." He had it in his mind to be pure in his dating relationships, but when his girlfriends put on the pressure, his resolve tumbled like a house of cards. He felt ashamed and wanted to keep it to himself. He was too proud to get help until it was too late. Sound familiar?

Jeff now knows that a physical standard should be made before dating ever begins. He also knows that the standard has to be for public record. His friends need to know, his pastor needs to know, and most important, his date needs to know. If your teen is already dating, you still need to discuss the limits and encourage your son or daughter to discuss the limits with dates. And even when both parties agree that sex is not an option, there are two overriding principles one must remember:

1. Always stay in control of your body (1 Thessalonians 4:3).

2. Always show respect for your body and your date's (1 Corinthians 6:20).

As you read through the next section on refusal skills and self-control, read it in such a way as to apply it, first in your own life as a believer in God, and then again as a parent or worker who wants to transfer these critical truths to someone you love.

The second lie for Jeff was, "I can quit whenever I want." Without accountability and encouragement, Jeff was a sitting duck. His history of explicit sex left him with intense curiosity and a spirit of entitlement. His image of "manhood" became warped. And without mentoring and confrontation, he was left to try to find a way out by himself. That's hard enough for us older humans, almost impossible for a 16-year-old young man.

Never make the mistake of believing that *your* children or *your* youth group is exempt from these kinds of temptations and behaviors. National surveys don't show much statistical difference in the sexual behavior of teens who go to church and those who don't. Church programs and school activities are good. They keep our teens involved in wholesome activities with appropriate supervision. But they are no

The national surveys don't show much statistical difference in the sexual behaviors of church-going teens and those who don't go to church.

substitute for a confidential adult mentor. Teens need guiding friendship and someone to believe in them. Approval is their number one developmental need during this time in their lives. It is not a question of whether they will seek approval, only where they will find it.

And here is an important truth-tip for any parent working through this book. As your child enters adolescence, there is a natural, God-designed dynamic that kicks in. *Your child is moving away from your guidance and influence.* We can't put it any truer or simpler than that. And here is the kicker: *This is a good thing!*

The job of adolescents is to test the teachings of childhood against real world experience, to see if they are really true. They *have* to do this to make the truth their own. Some do a better job of learning quickly, and through the mistakes of others. But make no mistake, all youth pull away, test the values of their families and then, if they make good choices, the Truth draws them home, stronger than ever.

That was the "truth" part; here is the "tip." Accept this fact and recognize that your personal influence will be different. Not over, but different. Your job now is to model truths in your everyday life. Let your children see that you don't just talk the talk, but you walk the walk. Let kids see that your lives work well, living committed to the values of Scripture and under the care of Jesus. Continue to tell the truth and model the truth, but remember that the effectiveness of lecturing your own teens is all but gone.

Here is a challenge for you. Become the mentor of someone else's teen. Insert yourself in the life of your neighbor's daughter or your son's best friend. Tutor or coach; instruct or invite; but get involved. Be the parental influence and mature friend in the life of a teen through Big

If you know a college student who can talk effectively about his or her dating life in high school, and will back you up on key points and values, this is a good time to ask for the story. Teens listen to college students saying the same thing you would say!

Brother/Big Sister, Scouting, Fellowship of Christian Athletes, Campus Life clubs or your church youth group. The opportunities are endless. And then pray that another caring adult will come alongside your child and mentor him or her, too.

WHEN TO SAY "WHEN!"

Here are five boundaries that parents (and youth workers) need to discuss *before* their kids start dating. Having a philosophy of dating and a well-defined set of values is indispensable to the dating health of your teen. Contrary to your feelings, teens listen to adults who love them. They just don't always show that they are listening! Our job is to find creative and effective ways to get our message across.

1. Delay dating.

Surveys and studies show that teens are more likely to remain virgins if they delay dating to 16 and even more likely if they delay dating to 18. On the inverse, teens who start dating and get sexually active at age 13 are likely to have, on average, eight sexual partners prior to marriage. A student who delays sexual activity until 18, on average, will have three sexual partners before marriage.

2. Don't drink and date.

It may seem obvious, but drinking alcohol does stupid things to your brain and to your will power and judgment—and to others you are with. Often a teen will say "Don't you trust me to be at a party and use good judgment?" Usually the answer is "I love you, and that is forever. I am your parent and my job is to protect you. I trust you, for the most part, but when alcohol is involved I do not trust the world around you." Don't drink and date! It is as deadly as drinking and driving!

3. Delay going steady.

The act of exclusive dating beings the process of "sequential monogamous relationships." Teens practice marriage by being in exclusive committed relationships, but they are generally short lived. The average dating relationship in the high school years lasts six weeks. This doesn't teach committed marriage, but that though breaking up is hard to do, it's okay and expected. After all, "Who stays married these days?"

4. Don't be alone; date in public.

Being in a setting with other people around adds protective factors to those who want to remain pure.

On a live call in radio talk show, I once had a teen call in saying, "I don't understand why my boyfriend and I are always getting into sex. We both have made a pledge to be pure, but it is not working. When we get alone in the **LINDA'S STORY** house and lie down on the couch together to watch a movie, it just seems it always becomes sexual. Is there something wrong with me?"

There is definitely something wrong with the boundaries!

> **Being alone**
> **+ Lying down**
> **+ Watching movies (especially sexually explicit movies)**
> **= Trouble keeping your pledge.**

You don't have to be a math major to understand this equation!

5. Do more double dating or group dating, but still be careful.

There is safety in numbers, usually. The forces of positive peer pressure can be put to good use on double dates or a group dating situation. The pressure is off to pair up, and all the great social and emotional good of getting to know others of the opposite sex are enjoyed, but the setting offers protections against sexual temptations.

Don't imagine, though, that this situation is safe all the time. There are too many horror stories where couples still pair off and alcohol gets involved. Coerced sexual experiences happen in this scenario all the time. Know who is going where and why!

SELF CONTROL AND REFUSAL SKILLS

Self-control is an interesting concept. Losing weight, saving money, exercise, doing the bills, keeping the house clean and the yard up all take self-control. You name it, it takes self-control. Self-control is making the choice to do the right thing, not the easy thing. The self-controlled person chooses right, not because someone else is forcing him or her, but because it is in the person's own best self-interest to do so. It is a fruit of the Spirit and Scripture tells us that we will reap a harvest if we do not give up in the struggle for righteousness (Galatians 6:8). God tells us, "Trust me, it is worth it!"

We have the wrong impression of how we attain self-control, as though it is just an act of the will. The truth is, no one can hope and strain and just try harder and then, all of a sudden—poof—find themselves to be perfectly self-controlled. Consider instead the idea of fruit on a tree. When the tree is in good soil, has quality water and plenty of sunshine, fruit naturally appears. The healthy tree doesn't strain and hope and decide that now is the time to make fruit. The fruit of the Spirit, including the fruit of self-control, is the result of abiding well in Christ, our True Vine (John 15). If you want to see self-restraint as a character trait in yourself and your family, first see that the prerequisite of having the abiding relationship with God is in place first. It all starts with being rooted in Christ above all else!

Self-control is not forged in the heat of battle. All good military professionals understand that soldiers capable of performing with courage, precision and self-control in war learned these disciplines months and years before they were called to the front lines. Self-discipline is not *absent* one minute and then *present* the next. It is nurtured and strengthened over time, first in easy situations then in more challenging ways. Soldiers learn first to obey, to follow through and to give their best effort. They prove it first in the small things like how they dress and march. Then when their skill and discipline is proven, opportunities to display that character open up in other aspects of life. It will be the same for you and the youth you love.

As parents we have the responsibility to teach self-control and self-discipline. Our strategy is to introduce our children to various habits and skills that will follow them into adulthood. Music lessons, meaningful household chores and limits on TV and music don't necessarily make

Self-control is not forged in the heat of battle.

parents the "good guys" in the short run. However, these disciplines when the tasks are relatively easy build the attitudes and character traits for life. Parents are to be parents first; friendship comes later.

Identify the circumstances that often send you out of control and the physical cues when anger or temptation is sneaking up on you. Part of self-control is taking yourself out of temptation's way before the situation develops. Teach your kids to make great decisions before the expected temptation occurs. Help them know their escape route even before trouble starts. If certain friends or places are typically troublesome, hotwire a "Plan B" into the situation by setting up code words for a phone call home or a certain number of rings at home designating a "help me get out of here" message. Don't leave your child's safety to an unsafe world!

THE FIVE WATCH-OUTS

Here are five simple ideas that you can introduce to your teens when you come upon one of those unpredictable teachable moments.

Watch out for the "lines." You know the drill. "If you loved me..." "A man has needs..." "I want to make you a man..." "Come on, everyone is doing it..." "I have protection..." and the beat goes on!

Lines are a sure sign of emotional blackmail and a guilt trip. If a person starts calling you names or trying to blackmail you, recognize *it is not* love. It is taking, not giving, and the person does not have your interests in mind!

Watch out for and be aware of your feelings. You're entitled to your opinion and your feelings. If it doesn't feel right, slow down. You know what being taken advantage of feels like. You may have to get yourself out of that situation. Just leave.

Watch out for alcohol. It deadens your senses and makes it difficult to think straight. Alcohol is the number one component of coerced sex. Don't drink and date!

Watch out for bad advice. Your friends don't know you like you know you. They may steer you wrong. The impression you get from TV and the movies is a lie. Don't believe it. Talk to people who know you and love you and want the best for you, like your parents, priest or pastor, school counselors or coaches. It is your life. Treat it like you are special!

Watch out for being alone with your date. Don't go to that room to talk. There is too much opportunity for something to go bad when you are all alone.

REFUSAL SKILLS PRIMER

Most likely, your teen has been through the "Refusal Skill Drill" in public or private school. These days it is regular health class material. Most parents, priests and pastors missed that class, though. Here is a brief refresher class that youth workers and parents may even find helpful in controlling the temptations of their own lives. Goodness knows we have our share of opportunities too.

The goals of knowing and using effective refusal skills are:

Keep your friends/job/spouse.

Have fun.

Stay out of trouble.

Stay in control.

There is a lot at risk, and learning to say "No" without losing a boyfriend or girlfriend is a great skill to have. Help your teens follow these tips.

1. Delay. You may not need this one every time, but it is helpful to know. "Let me get back to you on that." "I need to check with parents (boss, coach, etc.)."

2. Ask Questions. Be sure you know what you are being asked to do. "Where are we going?" "Who will be there?" "What will we be doing?" "Will there be alcohol?" "Will there be parents?"

3. Name the Trouble. Say that this is something you don't want to do. "I am not into smoking (drinking, R and X-rated movies, etc.)." "I am in training (studying, working, etc.)."

4. Name the Consequences. What could happen if you went against your better judgment? "I could lose my job (get kicked off the team, lose a scholarship, disappoint my parents). It is not worth it to me."

5. Suggest Realistic Alternatives. Suggest something fun and safe to do. Don't be condemning or judgmental. Offer ideas that you have done together in the past and enjoyed: sports, shopping, etc.

6. Move On. Get yourself out of this situation. "Call me when you are done." "I have to go now." "My ride is about here. Give me a call. Bye!"

As we strive to set up an environment where youth can grow up healthy and wise, it is critical that we develop a spirit of anticipation, a kind of sixth sense, when it comes to sensing what is "around the corner" for them. This is especially true when it comes to helping them navigate the sexual temptations that fill their world. We need to be sober and clear minded, because our adversary the devil is stalking them like a roaring lion, seeking an innocent and weak one to devoir (1 Peter 5:8).

Understanding intimacy, especially intimacy with God, is so important. Jesus says "Remain in me and I will remain in you" (John 15:4). This is the ultimate secret to a life of self-control and positive choices. It is much easier to convince your will to make good choices if you aren't surrounded by opportunities for disaster 24/7/365.

Encourage your teens to know the steps of intimacy and keep track of where they are in the process. Have your teens set do-able, concrete boundaries that they share with others. Communicate the non-negotiables of certain sexual activities that are to be reserved for marriage. Recognize the role of developing self-control as a process.

Simply yelling, "You have no self-control" doesn't really work.

As you convey the truths of refusal skills and self-control to your teens, consider being appropriately transparent about your own good choice and bad choices from your past. Don't brag and don't go too far in sharing all, but identify with your teens by telling part of your story.

Pray without ceasing, remembering that your teens are making thousands of choices a day, most of them terrific.

Praise them.

Protect them.

Forgive them.

Believe in them.

Discipline them.

Expect the best of them.

Make sure that these happen!

INTIMACY INVENTORY FOR MARRIED PARTNERS

Think about the meaning of intimacy that you would like your kids to learn. If you'd like, refer to a dictionary, read a book or article on the subject of intimacy, or check out the concept on the web. Completing this exercise will help you have a "real life" framework for talking about intimacy with your teen.

Stage One!

Question: Define intimacy in your own words: what behaviors, things, events or interactions do you most identify with intimacy?

Question: What three words would you say define intimacy for you?

Question: What three words would you say define intimacy for your spouse?

Stage Two!

Question: How has the nature of intimacy changed in your relationship since you first married?

Question: What do you remember was the most intimate part of your relationship when you first got together?

Question: What is the most intimate aspect of your current relationship?

Question: In terms of intimacy, what's changed, and why?

Question: What three new dynamics could help maintain or re-introduce intimacy into your relationship?

Stage Three!

Question: In what ways do you draw your spouse close, and consciously try to attract him or her? Think of two things you could do to draw your partner closer.

Question: What things do you do that push your spouse away? Think of two things you do to move away from your partner.

chapter nine

HOT
Topics

In 1989, the Eastern Soviet block began to cave in under the pressures of a failing economy and the attractiveness of democracy. In 1991, the juggernaut Soviet Union collapsed as well. The Cold War was over!

And with that emerging Glasnost, Christians around the world began to pray that the missionary opportunities that had been closed for so many years would now be open. Efforts to get Bibles into Russia sprang up everywhere. Short- and long-term missions groups began recruiting and training missionaries. Tentmaker ministries with English teachers and business leaders began to plan a move to the former Soviet Union. It was a time of great hope and optimism for evangelism.

At the same time as this openness represented a great opportunity for Christ, these same conditions represented an opportunity for Satan. Remember, any great opportunity or gift that God has given us can be polluted and destroyed by the evil one. So with these great plans for good, along came the greedy and immoral to take advantage. And evil such as the Russians had not known since the years of the despot Stalin came like a tidal wave across the continent.

Designer drugs and every form of alcohol came pouring in. Russia became the leader in trafficking women. International gambling and black markets took off. The country was unprepared for the prospect of so much lawlessness and immorality. With the import of Western culture came the infusion of Western immorality as well. There were no laws to govern the trafficking of women or to control the depravity of Internet porn. These evil exploits spread like a terrible deadly virus, with no cure in sight. Only victims.

One aspect of this cultural freefall is particularly chilling. A report from the Associated Press reveals that Russia, along with Indonesia, is becoming a world center for the production of child pornography. AP reports that in Moscow a child pornography ring works in connection with another pornography ring in Texas. The Russian child pornographers are grossing about $1.4 million *a month* and their operation is virtually unrestricted by Russian law. It does not distinguish between child pornography and pornography involving adults. Under Russian law, this demonic exploitation of children is treated as a minor crime," according to Dimitry Chepchugov, head of Russia's Interior Ministry. Chepchugov noted that even if the ten child pornographers now being investigated by Russian authorities are charged, they will receive "no more than two years in prison if convicted." Russian police officials complain about the legal chaos that has turned Russia into an international center of child pornography production. Says Chepchugov: "Unfortunately, Russia has turned into a world trash bin of child pornography." That's the Russian Minister of the Interior speaking.

Paul in his letter to the church at Ephesus gives a warning that seems prophetic for today.

Be very careful, then, how you live—not as unwise but as wise, making the most of every opportunity, because the days are evil (Ephesians 5:15, 16).

There is certainly great opportunity for good, and sadly an equally great opportunity for evil. For every champion of marriage there are so-called modernists propagating cohabitation. For each testimony of purity, others are selling porn. And for some reason the lines are getting less defined and increasingly gray. We live in a land of shadows, doubt and confusion. We live in a land of lies.

Certainly we recognize that there are difficult distinctions in our culture and no want for opinions of what is absolutely right and what is undeniably wrong. Sometimes it's hard to be sure. Our culture is complex and diverse. One person's ceiling is another's floor.

Yet God has called the Church to stand courageously and speak out against evil, to confront injustice and unrighteousness where we see it. Our country is only a few bad decisions away from joining Russia in this moral freefall.

English philosopher Edmund Burke said, "The only thing necessary for the triumph of evil is for good men to do nothing." It is time for the Church to take on the tough topics and to declare the truth. Jesus predicted that in the end times, "because of the increase of wickedness, the love of most will grow cold." Still he challenged us to persevere in the face of this terrible condition, noting that "he who stands firm to the end will be saved" (Matthew 24:12, 13).

How do you feel about the moral condition of our country?

__I feel so discouraged I can't move.

__I feel the resolve to be the one to make a difference.

__I just get tired.

__I tend to just look at my family and my needs.

__I am confident that God can make a difference and will.

__I pray. I don't know what else to do.

__Other _____

Is there really any hope?

HOT POTATOES AND TEACHABLE MOMENTS

Hot topics are controversial. The issues of sexual health and sexual behavior are by nature intimate and personal. They can be politically charged, such as the issue of abortion. They can be morally charged, like the issue of homosexuality. How these issues are approached can have a huge impact on our communities, our churches and our families. What will you say in a teachable moment with your son or daughter on which of these topics? Do you have an opinion you want to be emphatic about? Do you have some questions you'd like to challenge your teenager to think about?

There is a very real temptation to treat these hot topics like hot potatoes. Dads toss the potato saying, "Go ask your mom." Moms toss it back saying, "Wait till your dad gets home." Youth pastors say, "This isn't something we talk about here." Pretty soon children and teens come to believe that these questions are off limits. The very place teens should be going for answers seems to be off limits.

As caring adults we need to be able to see these issues not as hot potatoes but as teachable moments. Take into account what your youth is asking. If you are unprepared and not paying attention, it is easy to over-answer or under-answer an innocent question.

Here are some clues from children that they are ready to talk about one or more of these tender subjects:

- They begin to ask questions about images they see or things that they hear at school.
- They begin to make fun of words that they hear about such subjects as masturbation, or being gay.
- They begin to call their friends names like "homo," "gay," "sexy."
- They talk frequently about this subject matter to their friends in your presence.
- They ask you direct questions about these subjects.

You may wonder why you have to make your own decision on these hot topics. With all the subtleties on these issues, wouldn't it be smarter to rely on the pros? Theologians, psychologists, ethicists; wouldn't they know better than me?" you might ask. You would think if you put all these educated and dedicated people in one room they could come up with policies on sexual health that everyone can agree on. Think again! Not only would we not get a policy; there would probably be a fistfight of heavy weight proportions. There have been murders committed over the disagreements surrounding these issues. Just as the psychologists can't agree, many church leaders can't agree.

In some denominations these issues are splitting the church wide open. They are hot!

Here are some things to keep in mind as we get ready to come to terms with these important yet volatile issues:

1. As we have said all along, the lies surrounding sexual health are emotionally charged. Sometimes it feels as if the loving thing to do is to just ease up on the confrontation just to keep the peace. Satan loves this answer. If we do nothing, he can do anything!

2. "Reasonable people disagree." This is true. But don't jump to the conclusion that because reasonable people disagree, there is no true answer. Not only do reasonable people disagree, but they are often wrong.

3. Church policy may not be based on truth, but on traditions. Most denominations and many families are steeped in generations of tradition. Tradition is fine for many things: food style and holiday celebrations, for instance. But issues so important to God demand our deepest prayer and commitment to sound doctrine.

4. In a practical sense, these issues won't go away by ignoring them. People who stand for nothing fall for anything.

COHABITATION

Living together, cohabitation, as a lifestyle is on the rise. In the 60s and 70s about a half million unmarried persons were living together. By 1980 that number was 1.5 million. By 1990 the number was nearly three million. And by 2000 the number was almost five million.

Researchers estimate that today as many as 50% of Americans cohabit at one time or another prior to marriage. America also appears to be changing its attitude toward cohabitation. George Barna has reported that 60% of Americans believed that the best way to establish a successful marriage is to cohabit prior to marriage. Another survey found that two-thirds (66%) of high school senior boys agreed or mostly agreed with the statement, "It is usually a good idea for a couple to live together before getting married in order to find out whether they really get along."

Cohabitation is not the same as marriage. It is not recognized as marriage by the state. Participants are living together because it is their intent *not* to be married, at least for the time being. Some will say that a cohabiting couple is "married in the eyes of God," but that is not true. They are not married in God's eyes because they are living contrary to biblical statements about marriage. And they are not married in their own eyes because they have specifically decided *not* to marry.

Marriage is God's plan for intimate companionship for life (Genesis 2:18). It provides a context for the procreation and nurture of children (Ephesians 6:1, 2). And finally, marriage provides a godly outlet for sexual desire (1 Corinthians 7:2).

Sexual intercourse outside of marriage also has consequences. Writing to the church in Corinth, the Apostle Paul said that when a man joins himself to a prostitute, he becomes one body with her (1 Corinthians 6:16). The context of the discussion was a problem within

Cohabitation is not the same as marriage. Participants are living together because it is their intent *not* to be married.

the church. A man in the church was having sexual relations with his father's wife (1 Corinthians 5:1–3). Paul calls this relationship sinful. First, it was incestuous, which was condemned by the Old Testament (Levitucus 18:8; Deuteronomy 22:30). Second, there was no marital union, but instead an example of cohabitation. Paul's admonition to us is to flee sexual immorality (1 Corinthians 6:18).

Sexual immorality is condemned over two dozen times in the New Testament. The Greek word Scripture uses to describe sexual sin is *porneia*, a word that includes all forms of illicit sexual intercourse. Paul wrote:

> *It is God's will that you should be sanctified: that you should avoid sexual immorality; that each of you should learn to control his own body in a way that is holy and honorable, not in passionate lust like the heathen, who do not know God* (1 Thessalonians 4:3–5).

Living together outside of marriage not only violates biblical commands, but it puts a couple and their future marriage at risk.

Establish firm boundaries and expectations for your teens. The stronger your relationship and the stronger your resolve to communicate exactly what you believe to be holy and healthy, the greater chance your teens will pursue purity as a lifestyle.

What are your feelings about living together experiences?

What do you think are the greatest risks of experimenting with cohabitating?

PORNOGRAPHY AND MASTURBATION

Marcus gave his life to Christ when he was five. He and his family went

to church every week and as time went by his commitment to Christ grew. He went to camp in seventh grade and there rededicated his life and felt the Lord in his life more strongly than ever. That was a great year.

In high school, Marcus began to lead his church youth group and he got involved in mission trips. He joined the youth worship team and participated in the lead role of the Easter Celebration services.

The same year that Marcus rededicated his life to Christ was also a bad year. It all began in a normal way. He went over to his friend's house, where his friend pulled out a box of his dad's adult magazines. It began as simple pubescent curiosity. But the curiosity continued to grow.

While still in middle school, Marcus found out about Internet porn. Internet porn could take a visitor to a site of increasingly explicit sexual images and increasingly depraved sex. It was anonymous, so Marcus didn't worry so much about getting caught. The Internet also gave Marcus access to instant messenger services and that connected him to real people looking for a similar sexual charge. He began to have conversations with girls that were sexually explicit.

Marcus was terribly disappointed with this part of his dark side. He would go through stages where he disposed of all software and connections to the Internet sites that tempted him. He would dedicate himself to prayer and seek to be healed of this addiction. But in times of stress he would reload the programs and revisit the pornographic sites.

Then it turned even more real. Marcus began to have conversations that would lead to actually meeting the person on the other end of cyberspace conversation. They would meet and share sexual intimacies, and he would arrive home before his friends or family would realize he was gone.

Then it turned tragic. A young lady wanted to meet Marcus, and he agreed. She said she was 18. Marcus was 22 and she seemed a bit young for him, but he figured she was a legal adult. They met in a deserted parking lot and engaged in sexual behaviors. About that time the police drove up, interested in what a car was doing in a darkened parking lot. They were found out, and the girl told police that she as actually 16.

Marcus was horrified. He knew his addictions were wrong, but he never wanted to be a part of a young teen being drawn into this sadness.

It turned out the girl wasn't 16 after all. She was 14.

Marcus was arrested on child sexual molestation charges. He is now charged with serious sex crimes and may have to register under federal law as a registered sex offender.

He is sorry. Sorry for the pain he has caused his family and friends. Sorry for the way that this has impacted his ministry and God's reputation. Sorry for the way this may impact his future. He is especially sorry for hurting this young woman and her family. He is actively involved in counseling, and if he completes his treatment he will have opportunities to get on with this life.

I asked Marcus if during his time as a student in church anyone ever came and offered the kind of ministry that would have given him hope to get out of this addictive lifestyle. He said about once a year his youth pastor taught about the sin of sex outside of marriage, but there was never any message of hope for the addicted or a challenge to get help. He said, "I was so ashamed and felt so alone. I am not sure that even if I was offered help I could have accepted it. I wish someone would have come alongside me then. Then I wouldn't be where I am now. I am sure."

How does this story make you feel?

How do you usually feel about sex offenders?

During the 1980s, pornography experienced substantial decline in America. All of the recommendations of the Attorney General's 1986 Commission on Pornography were passed into legislation. Adult bookstores were pushed either out of town or to the perimeters of town in many communities and material harmful to children was regulated on a fairly consistent basis.

The porn industry has found a revival in cyberspace. Much of our entertainment industry is impacted by porn: the printed word, the television, the VCR and movies. And each of these areas of entertainment is exploited by the porn business. All the traditional pornography elements—porn book stores, live peep shows, and smut movies—have now set up shop online. Not only have those looking for pornography been able to tap into an endless supply online, but through e-mail and chat room advertising, the porn industry is recruiting thousands of viewers who never would have set foot into an adult bookstore.

DID YOU KNOW?

...that pornography consumption can be as mood altering and as addictive as narcotics? In fact, some studies have indicated that pornography can have the same effect on the brain as cocaine. Images can be permanently "burned" into the memory by epinephrine, a chemical in the brain.

... that according to Nielson NetRatings, 17.5 million people visited porn sites in January 2000? (*U.S. News & World Report,* 3/27/2000.)

... that there are more outlets for hardcore pornography in this country than there are McDonalds restaurants?

... that rape statistics are proportionately higher in those states with higher pornography sales and lower in those states with lower pornography sales?

... that cyberporn sales—including videos and accessories ordered online—accounted for 8% of 1999's $18 billion E-commerce pie? (*U.S. News & World Report,* 3/27/2000.) That's nearly $5.25 for every man, woman and child in the United States!

... that boys ages 12–17 are one of the largest consumers of pornography and pornographers target them for that reason. If the pornographers can arrange for the young person to become addicted, then a steady flow of income is assured.

(Information received from Enough is Enough, Morality in Media, and National Coalition for the Protection of Children and Families.)

Masturbation is typically accompanied by the use of pornographic material or sexual fantasy, especially in males. "Safer Sex" advocates have suggested "mutual masturbation" as an acceptable form of sexual behavior for non-married teens. These behaviors go against Scripture, which admonishes us to keep our minds, hearts and bodies pure from sexual sin. Masturbation can threaten to diminish the pleasure and intimacy of sex that God designed for married partners.

Masturbation and pornography have been shown to be addictive in nature, consuming the fantasy life of the user. Several sttudies show a four-step progression among many men who consume pornography.

Step One

Once involved in pornographic materials, people get hooked and keep coming back for more to get their sexual "turn ons." The material provides a powerful sexual stimulant or aphrodisiac effect, followed by sexual release, most often through masturbation. The pornography provides imagery which they frequently recall to mind and elaborate on in their fantasies.

Step Two

Second, there is an escalation in need for rougher and more sexually shocking material in order to get the same sexual stimulation as before. If their wives or partners are involved with them, they eventually push their partners into increasingly bizarre and deviant sexual activities. Their addiction and escalation are mainly due to the powerful sexual imagery in their minds, implanted there by the exposure to pornography. They often prefer this sexual imagery, accompanied by masturbation, to sexual intercourse itself.

Step Three

Third, over time there is a desensitization to the material's effect. What was first gross, shocking and disturbing becomes acceptable and commonplace. Material originally perceived as shocking, taboo-breaking, illegal, repulsive or immoral, though still sexually arousing, in time becomes acceptable or commonplace, regardless of previous moral beliefs and personal standards.

Step Four

And fourth, there is an increased tendency to start "acting out" the sexual activities seen in the pornography. What was first fantasy, in time becomes reality. What is viewed is first masturbated to at the fantasy level then later acted out in real life behavior. This nearly always disturbs the individual's marriage or psychological equilibrium.

Women addicted to pornography bear a certain stigma. Shame is common among pornography addicts, but especially among those who are female. After all, they are supposed to be prim and proper with no propensity for illicit behavior. Pornographers have always depicted women as the object of desire. Women are supposed to be the sought after, not the seeker. Or so society silently says.

Sadly, a lot of the pornography targeted toward women is produced by women—women who choose to victimize other women. Those

When your kids are old enough to spend time alone with friends without close adult supervision, be sure they know how to get themselves out of a situation that could be harmful.

producers understand the differences between the male and female brain and produce films with the female market in mind.

Women normally look at sex through the filter of romance and relationship, both forms of communication. They enjoy hugging and kissing, as well as other forms of physical closeness while men are seduced by the visual imagery of the sex act itself (whatever form it takes). Pornographers know these differences and have begun to produce porn films that include thinly veiled portrayals of relationships.

In his excellent book, *The Drug of The New Millennium: The Science of How Internet Pornography Radically Alters the Human Brain and Body*, author and researcher Mark B. Kastleman says:

Internet pornographers often use "average looking" females as their subjects so that the female viewer can more easily relate by fantasizing or imagining herself playing the role. Likewise, they portray both the male and female pleasuring each other equally... In essence, the Internet pornographers have taken the successful "soap opera/romance novel" genre and wrapped it around pornography in order to seduce the female viewer. It is critical that parents come to a point of comfort in order to discuss these issues with their children. Conversations with your counselor, priest, pastor, rabbi or other trusted spiritual/family advisor may also be helpful. When your kids are old enough to spend time alone with friends without close adult supervision, be sure they know how to get themselves out of a situation that could be harmful. If you shy away from this subject too much, their curiosity may get the best of them when a friend pulls out a magazine or video. And it happens at a younger age than most of us would like to think.[1]

ABORTION AND CONTRACEPTION

Abortion is a very hot topic. Up until 30 years ago virtually all denominations agreed that abortion was the equivalent of murder and was against the law. And there was virtual agreement that the plan of God was to bring life, not death. Scripture recognizes human life as a sacred gift of God. Only God has the right to determine when life begins. Abortion, though a *legal* option in our society, is not a *moral* option under Scripture. Abortion has become a worldwide social evil that significantly threatens the psychological, spiritual, physical and moral health of entire societies.

Abortion causes deep emotional, psychological and spiritual wounds for the mother, father, other family members and friends. Increasingly, the Body of Christ has become aware of post abortion issues and is designing ministries to help those who have been traumatized by abortion, communicating the forgiveness, healing and love of Jesus Christ.

It is important that parents and pastors are aware of the serious consequences to having an abortion. Pro-abortion advocates tend to downplay abortion as a simple medical procedure. And while for the most part, abortions occur without serious medical consequences, the complications can be serious and far-reaching.

Women who experience abortions tend to have an increased level of promiscuity and sexually transmitted diseases. Abortion complication is the fifth leading cause of maternal death in the United States. Two percent of women who have abortions suffer life-threatening complications, such as bleeding, fever and infection. Infection, including pelvic inflammatory disease, occurs in 30% of abortions; if not stopped soon enough, PID can leave a woman infertile. Ectopic pregnancies—pregnancies developing in the fallopian tube—are increasing because sometimes the uterus is scarred from an abortion. The fertilized egg, the zygote, cannot get into the uterus and implant. Complications such as uterine perforation, cervical laceration and placenta previa, not only can cause severe problems at the time a pregnancy is terminated, but can also lead to problems in future pregnancies, such as miscarriages, premature births, fetal deaths and children born with handicaps. Any problem or change with a woman's reproductive organs may affect the development of her future children. Women who have abortions have up to 127% higher risk for premature births in subsequent pregnancies; the rate is higher with multiple abortions.[2]

HOT TOPICS AND YOUR CHURCH

These Hot Topics are not the only ones out there. Your youth group should consider establishing a policy on what represents appropriate dating behavior and what represents appropriate dress. Confront the content of movies and TV shows and the issues surrounding the use of sexual innuendo—and course language, for the use of humor is important, too. Someone needs to speak out on the soft porn of romance novels and women's magazines that tell bold-faced lies to young women about the nature of love and marriage and commitment.

As a concerned parent and parishoner it is sometimes hard to know when to assert yourself and voice your concerns. Make it a matter of prayer. Talk to your small group or class and see if they feel the same as you and if they have any ideas. Together, with God's help, you too can bring these hot topics to a place where they can be confronted so that solid teaching and Spirit-led ministries can move ahead.

A growing body of research shows a definite link between abortion and breast cancer. The risk increases when a hormonally normal pregnancy is terminated before 32 weeks. Although abortion advocates picture themselves as being primarily concerned with women's health, they have covered up this information.[3]

Women who undergo abortions experience psychological consequences as well. Then tend to have a diminished respect for human life. Post abortion syndrome, a series of psychological effects experienced by 19% to 60% of women, range from mild depression to suicide or attempted suicide. They often experience overwhelming feelings of regret or guilt during later pregnancies. Flashbacks and nightmares haunt them.[4] Some women go into denial, instead of giving way to the natural motions of relief, followed by guilt, sadness and grief at the loss of the child.[5] Women who have had abortions experience more than 100 different psychological reactions including alcoholism, smoking, drug abuse, eating disorders, sexual addictions and self-destructive behavior.[6] Fathers of aborted children also experience feelings of guilt or regret.[8] (For web sites on the consequences of abortion see: http://afterabortion.org/.)

Why do you feel that many women who have had an abortion feel uncomfortable talking about their experience in Church?

Why do you think so many churches do not have a post-abortion healing ministry?

CONTRACEPTION DISTRIBUTION FOR THE NON-MARRIED

For over 30 years, "Safe Sex" educators have advocated for the distribution of contraceptives as a way of reducing unmarried pregnancies and sexually transmitted diseases. The results of these "Comprehensive Sex Education" designs and similar "Abstinence Plus" programs have been devastating. The implied message in many sex education programs is, "Since you cannot control yourself, at least use these contraceptives." Worth Waiting For disagrees with this philosophy and methodology.

Worth Waiting For does not distribute, promote or in any way encourage the use of contraceptives as a method of reducing sexual behavior or pregnancy rates in non-marital sexual behavior.

Contraception in marriage can also be a controversial topic. Some Christians see contraception as demeaning to women and as an interference in God's design for fertility. Married adults need to openly discuss their use of contraceptives. Some contraceptives cause spontaneous abortion of an embryo and others have profound health risks associated with them. Each couple should seek godly counsel and consult with their pastor or priest and medical professional before using contraceptives.

HOMOSEXUALITY

The subject of homosexuality is one of the most dividing subjects parents face. To have a son or daughter confess to struggling with homosexuality or embrace homosexuality as a lifestyle is one of the most troubling experiences a Christian family can go through. It cuts quickly to the tension between unconditional love and a commitment to the truth of Scripture. Again our study can only be very brief, but perhaps it will be enough to wet your whistle for more research and prayer.

The Old Testament specificially prohibits homosexuality and its practice of sodomy or anal sex.

Do not lie with a man, as one lies with a woman: that is detestable (Leviticus 18:22).

If a man lies with a man, as he lies with a woman, both of them have done what is detestable: they shall surely be put to death; their blood shall be upon them (Leviticus 20:13).

Leviticus 18–20 also have numerous commandments concerning various condemned sexual practices, including incest, adultery (sex between two married individuals not married to each other) and fornication (sex between unmarried individuals) and bestiality. God designed sex to be between a husband and wife in the context of marriage. This is the overriding principle.

New Testament Scripture is equally firm. When Christianity began its spread to the Gentile nations, the practice of homosexuality was not an unusual heathen temple practice. Paul had to specifically address this practice as various pagan religious thoughts began to creep into the religious life of the churches in Rome and Corinth.

Therefore God gave them over in the sinful desires of their hearts to sexual impurity for the degrading of their bodies with one another.

They exchanged the truth of God for a lie, and worshiped and served created things rather than the Creator—who is forever praised. Amen. Because of this, God gave them over to shameful lusts. Even their women exchanged natural relations for unnatural ones. In the same way the men also abandoned natural relations with women and were inflamed with lust for one another. Men committed indecent acts with other men, and received in themselves the due penalty for their perversion. Although they know God's righteous decree that those who do such things deserve death, they not only continue to do these very things but also approve of those who practice them (Romans 1:24–27, 32).

Do you not know that the wicked will not inherit the kingdom of God? Do not be deceived: Neither the sexually immoral, nor idolaters, nor male prostitutes, nor homosexual offenders, nor thieves, nor the greedy, nor drunkards, nor slanderers, nor swindlers will inherit the kingdom of God (1 Corinthians 6:9, 10).

Worth Waiting For believes homosexuality and homosexual marriages to be mentally, emotionally, physically and socially unhealthy, and forbidden spiritually.

At the same time, we also understand that some teens, young adults, their friends and family may struggle with issues of sexual identity and may find a traditional heterosexual marriage difficult. Celibacy, a permanent life-choice of sexual abstinence, is God's design for dealing with sexual conduct for homosexual and single adults.

It is critical to make one last point.

We have been discussing very important issues. But there is a distinct difference between an issue and a person. John Frey said it well in his book *Jesus, the Pastor.*

Issues are Issues. People are People. Issues need to be addressed. People need to be loved. Keeping out of the hurtful tangle of mixing people and issues takes a prolonged gaze at Jesus. He is the Master at keeping out of the ego-driven, moralistic, tangled mess that we often, with the best of intentions, make.[8]

Never forget Jesus' own words that he "came to seek and save the lost." Our job is to dance the fine line of telling the truth without judging the person. Behavior can be healthy or unhealthy, functional or dysfunctional, holy or unholy. But God loves all people without limits. We have all been bought with a cost.

chapter ten

HANDLING TEEN
Pregnancy
AND DISEASE

The physical consequences of sex outside of marriage are often lifelong and can be devastating. There is no reason for our children to suffer these consequences. Our children don't deserve to be pregnant outside of marriage. Our children don't deserve sexually transmitted diseases that can rob them of their ability to have children in a future loving marriage. We desire everything that is good for our children and the generations to come. But what if lives are stopped short due to ravaging disease such as human papillomavirus (HPV) or HIV? What happens then? What happens to a family when an unmarried teen becomes pregnant? Let's take some time to look at the very real physical consequences so we can be ready with the facts when we talk to our kids about these realities.

THE FACTS ABOUT TEEN PREGNANCY

Let's begin with some facts about teen pregnancy in the United States.

- Thirty-five percent of sexually active girls become pregnant at least once by the age of 20.[1]
- The United States has the highest rates of teen pregnancy and births in the western industrialized world.[2]

- About 840,000 teens become pregnant every year. One-third of these babies are aborted. Over 75% of teens giving birth are unmarried.[3]

Taking these statistics seriously is one of the most important jobs we have as parents. These are real facts with real consequences. Our sex-saturated society has done little to talk about the consequences of sexual activity, either for the teens involved or their families. When teens become pregnant outside of marriage, it affects everyone around the them, especially their families. They face choices that have long-term or even lifelong consequences.

The emotional part of pregnancy can be a surprise to all women, but especially to teens. The hormonal changes in the body during pregnancy cause emotions to run high! Adolescence is a time of super-charged emotions to begin with, and pregnancy makes the emotions even more intense. This can be confusing to the people around a pregnant woman and a source of tension with the dad. He needs to remember that she has a physical reason for being very emotional (hormones). Also, the fact that she carries the baby causes the mother to feel more pressure to make decisions for the future. At the same time, the mom has to realize the immense pressure put on the father of the baby. He is often seen as the villain

According to the *American Journal of Public Health,* "Men past school-age father two thirds of the children born to school-age mothers. These men average 4.2 years older than the senior-high mothers and 6.7 years older than the junior-high mothers."[4]

and needs her support to stay by her side. For these reasons, patience and understanding are in order on the part of all of the important people in the teen mom and dad's lives. This new life coming into the world will impact the mom and dad, both sets of grandparents, brothers, sisters, teachers, coaches, friends and virtually all others in the birth parents' lives.

Some decisions need to be made quickly upon learning of the pregnancy, and some can be processed for several months.

Will I have this baby?

This is one of the most important decisions of a young woman's life. Will the mom carry and deliver her baby or will she choose abortion? In the crisis of an unplanned pregnancy, the temptation is to make the problem "go away" quickly. Teenagers may see abortion as the way to keep their parents from learning about the pregnancy. After all, since Roe vs. Wade, the procedure is safe, legal and confidential. In the decades since Roe vs. Wade, millions of women have chosen abortion. And millions of women have lived with consequences that no one told them about ahead of time. Many women, especially teenagers, face this decision unaware of the profound and long-lasting emotional and psychological consequences of abortion. The death of a child is never easy, and some women never recover from the decision to abort.

> Caleb was a 15 year old who sat in church doodling on Sanctity of Life Sunday. The speaker was a nationally known presenter on sanctity of life issues who told her own story of having an abortion in college. Caleb's mother looked over to see what he was sketching and was amazed to see a detailed drawing of a baby in the womb. Caleb gave the drawing to the presenter, who still carries it in her Bible. That was the first time Caleb said, "I think it's wrong to kill a baby that God made."

One of the most controversial debates about abortion is whether this procedure is the killing of a human being or simply an extraction of tissue from the uterus. Christian crisis pregnancy centers can help young women understand what is happening inside their bodies and find an answer to this question. It is important to get counseling for everyone involved in this decision, including the birth mom and dad, the teens' parents, pastors and, perhaps, professional counselors to help them make a decision that honors God.

What does God say about abortion? While Scripture does not talk directly about abortion, two passages help us understand God's view of the life he created.

For you created my inmost being; you knit me together in my mother's womb. I praise you because I am fearfully and wonderfully made; your works are wonderful, I know that full well. My frame was not hidden from you when I was made in the secret place. When I was woven together in the depths of the earth, your eyes saw my unformed body. All the days ordained for me were written in your book before one of them came to be (Psalm 139:13–16).

You shall not murder (Exodus 20:13).

God gives life and values it. He knows all about us even before we begin to form into a human being. He had all of our days on earth planned even before we were conceived. These are awesome and powerful words about the wonder and mystery of life.

Stop for a minute and write your thoughts and feelings about Psalm 139:13-16 and Exodus 20:13.

How can these passages help you talk to your teen about abortion?

What about medical care?

One of the most important decisions is who will be the teen mom's health care provider? Many teen moms deliver safely and have healthy babies, but much depends on how quickly she accesses the health care system.

The teen mom needs to see a doctor or nurse midwife as soon as possible after learning of the pregnancy. One of the reasons teen moms have more complications than older women is that they tend to delay going for health care early in pregnancy, so they do not receive good prenatal (before birth) care. Another reason that she and her baby may have more health problems is because of nutrition. If a mom doesn't "feed" her baby and her own body with good food, they will both have a hard time developing properly. The teen mom herself is still growing and developing. Both the baby and the teen mom have special nutritional needs. The teen mom will also need to be checked for sexually transmitted diseases. These diseases can cause the premature delivery of the baby and permanent damage or death to the newborn. Doctors and nurses can spot problems in pregnancy quickly. They have numerous tools to help both the mom and her baby. Generally the earlier a problem is found, the easier it is to remedy. So getting a young mom to health care as soon as possible is very important.

> In 1996, the Robin Hood Foundation carried out a large and insightful study regarding teen moms, dads and the effects of single parenting on their children. The Medical Institute for Sexual Health wrote:
> According to the Robin Hood report *Kids Having Kids*:
>
> - Seven out of 10 adolescent mothers drop out of high school.
> - The long-term wage earning power of adolescent fathers is greatly reduced.
> - The teenage sons of adolescent mothers are 2.7 times more likely to spend time in prison than the sons of mothers who delay child-bearing until their early 20s.
> - The teenage daughters of adolescent mothers are 50% more likely to bear children out of wedlock.
> - More than 80% of single mothers under 18 years of age end up in poverty and reliant on welfare assistance.[5]

Should I consider adoption?

Will the teen mom and dad parent the baby or place the baby for adoption? Adoption agencies, sometimes called family service agencies, can be a valuable resource for decision making. The professionals at these agencies help the mom make the very best decision for herself and her baby. Trained counselors offer free services to help her understand her options. Counselors work long and hard to help the mom arrive at the best decision. Many single moms who receive counseling at an adoption agency do not place their babies for adoption. This is perfectly all right and there are no penalties if she does decide to keep and parent her baby. These agencies are one of a young mother's best resources for dealing with this heart-wrenching decision.

Here is one word of caution regarding plans for adoption. God gave women special hormones that cause them to love the growing baby intensely, even before the baby is born. And right after birth a woman can be very protective of the newborn baby. Even the mom with strong resolve has doubts about her decision to put the baby up for adoption in the early days following birth. One of the most important tasks of the people who love her is to support her decision.

I once worked with a teen mom for four months making sure that she had good counseling on whether to place her baby for adoption or keep the baby and single parent. Jennifer went to an excellent adoption agency where the counselors were second to none. I also worked with her as her Lamaze instructor, talking late after every class about her current decisions. After months of difficult decision making that included her family, the father of the baby and his family, everyone agreed on a choice.

LINDA'S STORY

The baby was going to be placed for adoption. Both Jennifer and her boyfriend started to pick out possible adoptive families from profiles. I attended Jennifer's delivery and she did excellently. She had taken good care of herself and had no complications, delivering a healthy eight-pound baby girl. She was absolutely gorgeous (both mom and baby!).

I returned two days later when Jennifer was scheduled to leave the hospital and sign the adoption papers. When I walked into her room her face was bright red and her eyes swollen from crying. Jennifer had tears streaming down her cheeks, but that can be normal for any mom two days after delivery. Then Jennifer began to tell me what happened the night before.

As she talked, she wept and her shoulders shook. She had been all ready to face this day when she would sign the papers and leave the hospital without her baby. And she could face it because her boyfriend and everyone else important to her agreed that this was the best decision for the baby. The adoptive parents were perfect and her counselor had been in several times in the past two days to talk with her. She felt peaceful and loving about her decision. But then came last evening.

A female janitor had come in her room the previous night and said that she looked really young to have a baby. Then the janitor asked why her baby wasn't in her room with her. When Jennifer told her that she was in the nursery because she was placing the baby for adoption the janitor started screaming at her.

"What kind of mother hates her baby enough that she gives her away?" asked the janitor, among other things. That was it. That was all it took for Jennifer to change her mind. She kept her baby and single-parented. After all of the good decision making by Jennifer and the people close to her, it was the janitor on the evening shift who made the final decision through condemnation. We need to protect our birth moms from those who would change decisions that, perhaps, God would not have them change.

One of the potential negative consequences of teen pregnancy is the reaction of friends. Socializing with friends is one of the most important parts of being a teenager. Typically when a girl gets pregnant, her friends vow to help her when the baby comes. When she delivers her baby, many times the friends make good on their promise and pitch in to help. But as the baby gets older and starts to move around and get into things, the help is less frequent.

Another difficult part of being a teen parent is that friends may not understand that a teen parent can't go out on a Friday or Saturday night at a moment's notice. Friends can get really aggravated about this and give up calling the teen parent. The teen mom has to plan for a babysitter. She also has to be in early, so she has energy to be up with the baby during the night and to get the baby ready for childcare in the morning before school or work. After she has the baby, her life is totally different from that of her friends. She has responsibility for someone other than herself. This often leads to feelings of isolation, because her friends just can't understand her new needs.

Many cities offer support groups for teen moms that can be emotional lifesavers. They can connect her with organizations and services that will help her in her new life role. To find such groups, check with Pregnancy Resource Centers, adoption agencies, social service agencies and hospitals.

Talk frankly with your teenagers about the realities of pregnancy. It's a real risk of sexual activity, and one that changes multiple lives forever.

If your daughter has become pregnant or your son has fathered a child, this is not the time to say "you should have...." Remind yourself and your child that love is always given. Continue to give it even in this difficult circumstance. Remind yourself and your child of God's forgiveness and grace. See it now. Walking with your child through painful times will allow you both to participate in solid decisions that honor God.

THE FACTS ABOUT DISEASE

Pregnancy becomes obvious. Disease doesn't always. Millions of teens contract sexually transmitted diseases every year and no one ever knows, including their parents. Many don't even know themselves. Talking about STDs in a candid way could save your child's life.

HIV/AIDS receives media coverage and research attention, as well it should because of its seriousness. But it is not the only sexually transmitted disease that teenagers today face. Many diseases have serious health risks. These diseases are often without symptoms and spreading in epidemic proportions among our youth. The lies and myths associated with them still prevail. Even our medical doctors have trouble keeping up to date on research.

Americans are currently infected with an estimated 68 million infections of STDs. More than 15 million new infections occur each year. The two most common STDs, which are herpes and human papilloma virus (HPV), account for 65 of the 68 million current STD infections.[6] About 12 million people in the United States are infected with an STD each year and three million of these people are teenagers.[7] Adolescents and young adults (15–24) are the age groups at the greatest risk for acquiring an STD. Approximately two-thirds of all people who acquire STDs are under 25.[8]

When many of today's parents were teenagers, there were two major STDs. Where did we get our information? Most of us had some instruction in junior high gym class. A few of us had some sort of health course in high school. But we mostly shared information among friends. Television didn't talk about these topics. Personal computers didn't exist, nor did MTV. We were pretty much on our own to figure it out.

Where do teens today get information about STDs? Teens almost always answer "media." Teens today have access to almost unlimited information on the Internet. Unfortunately there are good and bad sources on the Internet and it's difficult for teens and adults to sort good from bad. Radio, television, cable television, satellite television—all have almost unlimited sources of sexual content.

Other answers to this question from teens is friends, school, doctors, movies and magazines. Once in a while the word "Mom" is offered as a source of information on sex and STDs. The word "Dad" almost never comes up—and this is very sad. Dads who are called to be the leaders of their families almost never talk to their teens about sex and the consequences.

CAN DOCTORS CURE STDS?

There are three main categories of STDs:
- infections with bacteria,
- viruses,
- other organisms.

Sexually transmitted disease is usually in the form of a virus or bacteria, but there are also many forms that do not fall into these two categories. Doctors treat bacterial infections with antibiotics and these are usually curable. However, some strains of bacterial STD, including some forms of gonorrhea, are not curable with certain antibiotics. One STD, Hepatitis B, now has a vaccine to prevent contracting it in the first place.

Teens, especially female teens, are much more susceptible to STDs than adults. The reasons for this increased susceptibility are:

- They are more likely to have multiple sexual partners.
- They may be more likely to engage in unprotected intercourse.
- Female adolescents have a physiologically increased susceptibility to some STDs including chlamydia.
- During the past two decades the age of initiation of sexual activity has steadily decreased and the age of first marriage has increased.[9]

The information on pages 164–169 gives you the facts on major sexually transmitted diseases, including chlamydia, genital herpes, gonorrhea, hepatitis B, human papilloma virus (HPV), syphilis and HIV/AIDS. Use this information to be ready to talk with your kids and give them information that they can trust.

DO CONDOMS PROTECT AGAINST STDS?

The Centers for Disease Control and Prevention (CDC) stated in 1997 that condoms had to be used consistently and correctly to be effective against sexually transmitted disease. They stated, "What does consistently and correctly mean? Consistently means using a condom every time you have sex—100% of the time—no exceptions. Correctly means following these steps...."

Many adults do not use condoms "consistently and correctly." To think that a teen will use anything correctly and consistently is almost ludicrous. But another report released in 2001 was perhaps one of the most important reports regarding the effectiveness of condoms to prevent disease.

"...The report was a result of a June 2000 workshop cosponsored by the U.S. Agency for International Development, the Food and Drug Administration, Centers for Disease Control and Prevention and the National Institutes of Health, in which the panel reviewed peer-reviewed studies to determine the effectiveness of condoms in reducing the spread of sexually transmitted diseases...In a July report, the panel confirmed that correct and consistent use of condoms can reduce the risk of HIV/AIDS and can prevent men from acquiring gonorrhea from women. However, the panel, led by the National Institutes of Health, concluded the epidemiological evidence is currently insufficient to determine the effectiveness of condoms in preventing the spread of chlamydial infection, syphilis, chancroid, trichomoniasis, genital herpes and genital human papillomavirus infection."[10]

After 40 years of the U.S. educational and health systems teaching that condoms are effective in preventing STDs, research shows that they are only effective against the spread of HIV and gonorrhea spread to men from women. This research states that there is no current evidence that condoms effectively prevent the spread of other STDs. There, undoubtedly, will be much research and debate in the future over this vital topic.

WHAT ABOUT AIDS?

Kansensero, Uganda is widely believed to be the birthplace of AIDS. It was in Kansensero and then in neighboring villages of the Rakai District of Uganda that the modern global AIDS pandemic took off sometime around 1973. International medical experts estimate 80 percent of the town's 12,000 remaining residents are now HIV-positive.

Statistics paint a sobering picture of what AIDS has done worldwide. It has already killed 18.8 million people and infected another 34.5 million—some 85 percent of them Africans, according to the United Nations AIDS Programme. Every one of the 45 sub-Saharan countries has some degree of infection, but in 16 countries the rates exceed 10 percent and in seven countries more than one out of five adults are HIV positive.

Several factors contribute to the swift rise of the HIV-AIDS pandemic in Uganda and Sub-Saharan Africa.

- The sharing of infected blood that is common in war-torn areas.
- Poor medical care and inadequate sterilization of needles due to poverty.
- A lack of professional health care and myths and misconceptions surrounding catching and curing AIDS.
- Predatory sexual treatment of women in male-dominated cultures.

These factors combine for a kind of "Perfect AIDS Storm" and the consequences are grave.

There are two additional reasons that the pandemic is out of control across Africa and these reasons are usually not addressed. One is that international and African church leaders have largely ignored the epidemic and failed to lead or show compassion. Secondly and most tragically, experts from around the world have sold the continent a bankrupt policy of condom distribution as the last-best-hope for salvation.

There is some hope—very bright hope. Uganda, the birthplace of AIDS, may be on its way to wiping it out. By returning to the traditional church family values of abstinence before marriage and fidelity in marriage, urged on by courageous leadership that did not buy the condom "safer-sex" lie, Uganda has succeeded in taming the virus. According to an academic study commissioned by the U.S. Agency for International Development (USAID) and released July 2002, the country of 24 million is "considered to be one of the world's earliest and best success stories in overcoming HIV." In this study, abstinence education has shown significant effectiveness in reducing AIDS in Uganda, with the HIV infection rate dropping 50 percent between the years 1992 and 2000.

Some have tried to credit condoms for the improvement. Dr. Edward C. Green, of the Harvard Center for Population and Development Studies, does not.

Dr. Green, who researched the Ugandan phenomenon with scientific objectivity stated, "Many of us in the AIDS and public health communities didn't believe that abstinence or delay, and faithfulness, were realistic goals. It now seems we were wrong."

When Ugandan President Yoweri Kaguta Museveni began to enlist help from religious organizations in 1992, many secular AIDS workers thought abstinence education programs would have few, if any, measurable results. Most policy-makers believed abstinence education to be not just a waste of time, but dangerous.

According to Dr. Green, HIV prevalence rates dropped 70 percent between 1991 and 2001. Uganda became the only country in the world that has seen any significant drop in AIDS infection rates. And abstinence education was at the core. When Ugandans were asked in surveys to identify the main action they have taken to avoid AIDS, faithfulness is the overwhelming first response in all groups except ages 15–19. In that age group, the first answer was abstaining or delaying sexual activity, closely followed by faithfulness.[11]

The Uganda AIDS Commission policy specifically recommended the following steps, and condom use was not listed among the commission's recommendations:

- Seek prompt treatment for any STD (sexually transmitted disease) infection and have regular check-ups.
- Have self-confidence and esteem skills as a method of preventing AIDS.
- Practice safe behavior, which involves:
- Abstaining from sex before and outside of marriage.
- Avoiding drugs and alcohol.
- Avoiding people who are bad influences.

While condom usage was encouraged for those who "would not practice abstinence," Dr. Vinand Nantulya, an infectious-disease specialist, pointed out in his analysis of the Uganda plan: "Ugandans never took to condoms."

The "Perfect AIDS Storm" is not over but God has shown us a way out! The question is, will we have the courage, character and leadership to choose well?

Teens in North American can learn from what happened in Uganda. Condoms didn't stop the rampage of AIDS. More people choosing to abstain from sex outside of marriage has helped to curb the disease in that country. When you have a teachable moment, tell the Uganda story. Find out what your son or daughter thinks about the real facts.

HELP! MY CHILD HAS AN STD

This is a difficult time for a parent. Depending on your awareness of your child's behavior, you may not even have known that he or she was sexually active. As a parent you'll be feeling all sorts of emotions: sadness, anger, guilt, fear and no doubt great disappointment. All of those emotions are real and strong.

When you confront your teenager remember: *He or she has the same set of emotions!* Most likely your teenager is also very afraid of losing the love and trust of Mom and Dad. He or she is scared and perhaps angry, too. If your child contracted a disease from the first sexual relationship he or she had, they may have been made to believe they "were the first" for their sexual partner, and now they know that is not true. Emotions in this setting run high. Your best friend at this moment is the truth, and your mind will work best if you are controlled by God's Spirit.

If you find yourself in this situation:

First consider getting a second medical opinion. Make sure that a full set of tests is done. Sometimes tests are wrong and sometimes tests find one disease but fail to pick up a second infection. Get good information. Also consider have your teen tested again every six months to a year. Sadly, some diseases take months or even years to show up in medical tests.

Be in prayer and be in conversation with your spouse if possible. Work through your issues as best you can first, so that you come to the meeting with your child with an attitude of healing and hope.

Have a good conversation with your child. If you need a facilitator to help you, make this investment. Your pastor or a trusted deacon or elder at your church may be just the person. Focus on the problem and avoid all kinds of guilt trip phrases that will block conversation ("What were you thinking?" "How could you do this to us?" "Do you know that you just ruined your life?" "What will others think of you/us?") None of these help!

Read up on the disease that has been diagnosed. While it may be scary, getting the best information possible will help in the long run. Get trusted advice, not just from the Internet, but trusted Internet sources. See our website at Worth Waiting For (www.worthwaitingfor.com) or visit www.themedicalinstitute.org.

Also remember this is not the end of the world. There are very good medical treatments that can cure many of the diseases. Some cannot be cured but can be treated very well. It is a hard time, but these are times that can mend and deepen relationships if you allow God to do his work.

Slow down. Give God a chance to do a miracle in all your lives, a miracle of love and hope.

WHAT CARING PEOPLE DO

All of this discussion has been about unplanned pregnancy disease, the prevalence of the epidemics and the death and destruction of worldwide AIDS. What is a caring person supposed to think? A thinking person is supposed to care!

God is asking us to get involved. God is asking us to go M.A.D! To go Make A Difference! We are promised tribulation in this world. We can go to the bank on that truth. But we are also promised that ultimately Jesus has overcome this world and its troubles. And he promises his presence with us always. So make a promise to yourself. Find out if your church is doing any AIDS ministry in your community, and if they aren't, help start one. Volunteer at a Crisis Pregnancy Center. Give of your financial resources to any of the dozens of international Christian ministries with projects that help in crisis pregnancy situations or offer medical care to victims of these diseases. Pray for nations ravaged by disease. Pray that workers would be released for the coming harvest!

Now that you know the truth about the consequences of sex outside of God's design, you are officially deputized as part of the solution! Time to get busy!

Chlamydia

Chlamydia is an infection that is caused by the most common bacterial sexually transmitted disease in the U.S. You can get it by vaginal, oral or anal sex. This bacteria infects primarily the uterus, fallopian tubes and ovaries of the female. In the male it can infect the epididymis and urethra, causing him to become sterile. Studies show that 8–25 percent of all college students have this bacterial infection. Teens have two or three times more chlamydia than adults. If you don't treat this infection, up to 30 percent of females will experience pelvic inflammatory disease (PID). PID can lead to ectopic pregnancy (the baby is growing in the fallopian tube instead of the uterus), infertility (inability to get pregnant when you want to) and chronic pelvic pain.

One of the most tricky parts of this disease is that as many as 75% of females and 25% of males who have it don't even know it; this disease is often asymptomatic (a disease with no symptoms). If symptoms do exist they can include abnormal genital discharges and burning with urination. Females may also experience lower abdominal pain or pain with intercourse. Males can experience swelling or pain in the testicles.

An ectopic pregnancy is dangerous. This means that the fallopian tube is blocked because of PID, so the fertilized egg cannot move through the fallopian tube to the uterus. The tube is too small to hold the pregnancy, and after three to four weeks it may rupture. This results in massive blood loss, or hemorrhage, and is the leading cause of death among pregnant teens.

Chlamydia is one of the leading causes of sterility. If a female is infected, she has a 25 percent chance of sterility, so she won't be able to get pregnant later when she wants to. After four infections there is close to a 100 percent chance of sterility.

The way to treat chlamydia is to take antibiotics. This is a curable disease, but only if the sexually active person goes to a doctor or a clinic to be tested for this disease on a regular basis and is treated with medication. If you don't treat this disease, it can also have devastating consequences on an unborn or newborn baby including premature birth (born too soon), infant pneumonia and eye infections.

Genital Herpes

Genital herpes is an infection from a virus. You can get this virus by direct sexual skin-to-skin contact with the area that is infected on the skin. This could happen during vaginal, anal or oral sex. The beginning symptoms may be very mild and include itching or burning sensations, pain in the legs, buttocks or genital area or vaginal discharge. In males, blisters or painful open sores may appear on the penis, scrotum or anus. In females the blisters and sores may appear on the vulva, inside of the vagina, on the cervix and in the anal region. Herpes can infect another person even if blisters are not present. This makes it very hard to know if your partner is infected.

The herpes virus does not live in the area of the body where it first infects the body. It invades the body and travels along the nerves and lodges itself into the nerve cells near the spinal cord. Periodically the virus moves down the nerves to the genitals and causes a new outbreak.

There is no cure for herpes. However, a doctor can prescribe medication to help to decrease the suffering from this disease.

One of the most devastating consequences of herpes is that it is a life-long disease. Sores appear and disappear throughout life, especially during times of stress. Outbreaks tend to occur when you least want them, such as during final exams, preparation for a wedding or on a vacation when you want to wear a tight swimsuit.

An increased risk with this disease is HIV. Open sores increase the risk of a person contracting HIV. Risks during pregnancy include premature delivery, death or serious brain damage to the newborn.

Gonorrhea

Gonorrhea is a bacterial infection that spreads by vaginal, anal or oral sex. In order to be exposed to gonorrhea, the male has to ejaculate. Like chlamydia, some people may not know they have gonorrhea because they have no symptoms for days or months after exposure. It is very infectious. If you have sex just one time with an infected person, you have a 40% chance of contracting the disease. Beginning symptoms are mild and appear within 2–10 days after having sex and being exposed. Symptoms include a pus-like discharge from the penis, vagina or rectum with burning or itching during urination. Sometimes it may be impossible to urinate because it is so painful.

When gonorrhea infects the uterus, fallopian tubes and ovaries in the female, she has pelvic inflammatory disease (PID). The pus from this disease can cause these organs and the intestines to stick together causing intense abdominal pain. She can also become sterile from the scars of the infection. Scarring can also happen in males, and if it's severe the male may not be able to urinate. Plastic surgery may be needed to rebuild his urethra.

This infection is usually successfully treated with antibiotics from a doctor. One big concern with this organism is that it resists penicillin. This means that treatment for gonorrhea may be increasingly more difficult.

Sometimes gonorrhea can have serious consequences on other parts of the body when the bacteria invades the bloodstream. All babies in the U.S. have their eyes treated with silver nitrate or an antibiotic shortly after birth to prevent blindness from gonorrhea.

Hepatitis B (HBV)

Hepatitis B is one of the most common STDs in the world today. This infection is caused by an extremely infectious virus that spread through blood, sexual secretions and saliva.

This virus attacks the liver and is severe enough to be fatal. Hepatitis B with symptoms include yellowing of the skin and whites of the eyes, tiredness, nausea, fever, headache, muscle aches, loss of appetite, vomiting, diarrhea, dark urine and gray-colored stools. Or you can be a carrier of the disease and not know that you are transmitting it to all of your sexual partners. Thirty-three percent of people with this virus are asymptomatic (they have no symptoms but can pass the disease to others).

The only cure for the disease is rest. Most infections clear up on their own within four to eight weeks. Some persons may become chronically infected leading to cirrhosis of the liver, liver cancer and immune system disorders. Pregnant women can transmit the disease to their unborn children and 90% of the infected infants become chronic carriers and are at risk for liver disease and liver cancer. In these children, 40–50% will develop cancer of the liver.

Doctors give a vaccine in three parts to prevent Hepatitis B. Many schools now require this for students who enroll.

Human Papilloma Virus (HPV)

HPV is a virus that spread by vaginal, anal or oral sex. This virus grows in moist places and mixes with sexual secretions to live easily on moist skin. You can get it just by skin-to-skin contact, even without sexual intercourse. This is one disease where condoms give very little protection; touch is all that is needed to spread this virus. Both males and females may have the disease but not have symptoms for months. This means that it can easily spread by sexual activity even when a person doesn't know he or she has the disease.

About 33–45 percent of sexually active single people are infected with HPV. It grows better in the female than the male. It lives easily in the female's vagina and on her cervix. The symptoms include painless fleshy, cauliflower-like warts on the outside and inside of the genitals, anus and throat. There is no known cure for this disease, but the warts may be treated in painful procedures by chemicals, freezing, laser therapy and surgery.

The most serious complication of HPV is that it is strongly associated with cervical cancer, as well as cancers of the vulva, vagina, penis and anus. OB-GYN News (vol. 24, no. 6), a magazine for health professionals, stated that HPV infections kill far more women in the United States each year than AIDS does. About 8,000 females die annually from HPV associated genital cancers. Teenage girls are much more likely to contract HPV than adult females; their bodies are more susceptible to the disease.

Babies exposed to the virus in the birth canal can develop warts in the throat which can obstruct (close off) the airway. Multiple surgeries may be necessary to remove the warts and can cause permanent scarring of the baby's vocal cords.

Syphilis

Syphilis is a bacterial infection transmitted by vaginal, anal or oral sex. It can also be spread non-sexually if a person comes in contact with the sores associated with this disease from an infected person. This disease passes through several stages including: incubation, primary, secondary, latent and tertiary. In the early phase of the disease, sores known as chancres appear on the genitals or on other parts of the body. These chancres are painless and will disappear on their own. This is one difficult part of syphilis. This first phase of syphilis usually occurs 10 days to three months after exposure to the bacteria. Each stage ends and symptoms disappear even if the person is not treated with medication. Unfortunately the infected person is getting sicker as time continues.

Secondary syphilis develops in six weeks to six months following the initial infection. Symptoms now include headache, fatigue, low-grade fever, skin rash and enlarged lymph nodes. A rash also appears on the body. These symptoms will also eventually disappear even without treatment and a latent period (a time when nothing seems to be happening) will follow, lasting from several months to 20 years.

Tertiary syphilis produces devastating problems in any other parts of the body, including aneurysms of the cardiovascular system, deterioration of the central nervous system, involvement of the bones and damage to peripheral nerves. Death can even occur due to these serious consequences.

Treatment for syphilis is penicillin and it is 100% effective. A doctor can prescribe another antibiotic for people who are allergic to penicillin.

If this disease is untreated in a pregnant woman, it can spread to the baby; the baby may be born dead or die shortly after birth. Of the babies who survive the pregnancy, 15 percent will die within the first month after birth. Of the rest of the babies who survive, one-third will have permanent abnormalities that may include obstruction of the nasal passages, enlarged liver and spleen and eye or ear damage.

HIV/AIDS

As of the end of 2002 there were 980,000 adults and children estimated to be living with HIV/AIDS in the United States and 42 million worldwide.[12] AIDS stands for a condition called Acquired Immunodeficiency Syndrome. It is a disease process that inhibits the immune system from fighting infections of all kinds. People die of multiple diseases that normally their immune system would fight. AIDS is caused by a virus called HIV which is the acronym for Human Immunodeficiency Virus.

HIV is transmitted *only* when the virus comes into direct contact with someone's bloodstream. This can happen primarily in four ways: through sexual intercourse, by using infected needles and syringes to inject intravenous drugs or steroids, from an infected mother to her unborn baby, or by receiving infected blood or blood products.

When a person is infected with HIV, the virus will be present in one or more of his or her bodily fluids. The bodily fluids most likely to contain HIV are blood, semen, vaginal secretions, and breast milk.

The early symptoms of HIV infection are similar to symptoms that accompany common illnesses. The difference is that the symptoms of HIV infection will last much longer and be much more severe. For instance, having diarrhea is not uncommon, but people infected with HIV may have diarrhea very frequently with no apparent cause. Swollen glands are a common symptom of having the flu, but having swollen glands in several parts of your body for no reason may be a symptom of HIV infection. Common symptoms of HIV infection are shown below:

- Very high fevers (over 103 degrees) that last for more than three to five days.
- A cough that brings up fluid from the lungs and lasts several weeks.
- Purplish blotches on the skin that are not the result of contact with irritating chemicals.
- Sores and infections that will not go away even after medical treatment.
- Tiredness or weakness that lasts for many weeks without explanation.
- Lymph nodes in at least two sites on the body that are swollen to marble-size or larger.
- Rapid weight loss (10 pounds or more) that is not the result of dieting.

- Painful or thick whitish coating in the mouth, or rectum with no apparent cause.
- Repeated colds, flu or flu-like symptoms that last for days at a time and recur frequently.
- Frequent diarrhea that has no apparent cause.

Because AIDS has only been studied for less than two decades, it is hard to say if all people diagnosed with full-blown AIDS will die. Because of HIV's long incubation period, it is hard to even know who has HIV. The longest an AIDS patient has survived is 17 years. But because AIDS information is becoming more readily available, people are getting tested sooner and starting treatment sooner. And as new treatments are developed, people with AIDS will live longer and healthier lives.

consequences AND Healing

How many teenagers do you know who do a good job of thinking ahead?

Most teens live in the present, in the particular moment. Future consequences of choices they make now, from academic performance to choice of friends to sexual relationships, are the furthest thing from their minds. Parents rant and rave and tear their hair out trying to get kids to see the connection between "If" and "Then." Then some of us just put our heads in the sand and wait for adolescence to be over.

When it comes to their sexual health, it's far more difficult than teens imagine to undo poor choices, even when they try.

As a therapist for more than a dozen years, I had seen quite a bit. Eating disorders, broken and breaking marriages, borderline personality disorder, alcohol addiction. Teens referred by the courts for theft. Young people recovering from a death in the family. Children recovering from abuse. Still, I was a bit surprised when Paul walked into the room.

I had seen Paul around church for about three years. He was thirty-something, successful, recently married for the first time to Staci. They

were the talk of the church. Staci and her family had attended this church all their lives. She was a graduate of a Christian college and was now an elementary school teacher. Before she met Paul she practically never dated. She was articulate, funny, involved in the community and had the looks and composure of a beauty pageant contestant. Staci and Paul dated for a bit over a year and their marriage was a first class celebration. Staci was obviously in love. She glowed when she was on Paul's arm. They were teased that they looked like "Barbi and Ken." And they did!

Paul started slowly. We spent four sessions talking about his childhood, his work, his somewhat recent conversion to Christ and how far he had come in his walk in only a few short years.

I finally got tired of the cat and mouse game. I took a risk. "Paul, you have been coming here for a month and I have yet to see anything that seems like a big issue for you. If you feel like you can trust me, why don't you just tell me what is going on?"

Paul looked down at the floor. He took several moments to compose himself. "I know I can trust you," he started, "but it is still kind of hard to talk about." Quiet again.

"Does it have to do with Staci?"

"No, no, she's great. She really loves me and we are so happy."

"So, what's up?"

Paul began. "Staci and I started dating about two years ago. She was so beautiful and I was surprised she was interested in me. I had been a Christian only for a couple of years and she has been one all her life. I didn't want to ruin it, so early on I talked to her about some boundaries for our dating relationship. You know, physical boundaries, things that we could do without being tempted to sin, and things that we couldn't do. She was great. She already had real clear boundaries, but I think it was the first time that a guy had ever brought up the subject with her. I felt like it gave our relationship power and peace at the same time. With the physical limits in place, we started doing all kinds of other things. We started reading plays together. We did some volunteer work together while we were dating. I spent a boatload of time with her brother and her parents. We started keeping prayer journals and sharing them with each other. We did really great." He stopped for a minute and I struggled not to fill the silence.

When he gathered himself he smiled and started up again. "When we got married we had kept our pledges to each other completely. I could tell that Staci was pleased. She told me that if I could control myself before we got married, that she would make me glad I did after we were married. She has kept her promise." We both laughed. After a time it got quiet again.

"So, Paul, I'm having a hard time seeing where the issues are for you. You married the woman of your dreams, you behaved like a gentleman during your courtship, and you have family and friends that believe in you and Staci. Help me understand how I can help."

"Before I met Staci, before I came to Christ, before I came to this church, I was a different guy. I was out of control and did a lot of drinking and dating, especially when I was in college, but even for eight to 10 years after that I did a lot of stupid things. Even though Staci was a virgin on our wedding day, I wasn't. I had been with lots of girls before I became a Christian. I really didn't know any better."

He got quiet again. I tried to connect with what I thought might be the problem. "Paul, does Staci know about your history?"

"Oh, sure, she knows everything." Paul looked right at me, "When I came to Christ everything for me changed. I quit drinking altogether and I never touched a girl again. I went back to school and got my Masters in Business. She knows that I made mistakes and she has forgiven me. I know that God has forgiven me."

Paul continued. "Here is the deal. As beautiful as Staci is, as in love as we are, when we are in bed together I cannot seem to get those other girls that I slept with out of my mind. I would give anything to change my past, but I can't. And I can't get them out of my mind. This part Staci doesn't know. I was hoping you could help me just make it go away. Can you help me?"

**How would you feel if you were in Paul's place?
How about Staci's place?**

**Do you think Paul has an obligation to talk
to Staci about what is going on?**

How do you imagine Staci will feel if Paul confides in her?

Paul's early choices had far reaching consequences—ones that he could not predict. On the surface, his life was great. Beneath the surface, he was miserable. When we talk to our kids about sexuality, we have to be ready to talk about what lies beneath the surface. Kids who have been sexually active may already be suffering from psychological, emotional, social or spiritual consequences of their choices.

PSYCHOLOGICAL CONSEQUENCES

Psychological consequences affect the mind. They change the way we think about life and its circumstances. Many psychologists believe that everything that goes into your mind, every image, thought, sound, is filed away in some short- or long-term memory file. Some disagree that *everything* is filed, at least filed well enough to find again. Many believe that an unconscious mind serves as kind of an "archive" of memories. In office terms these would be files stored in boxes and piles, unmarked and undated and hardly very useful.

This unconscious memory serves a useful purpose. Difficult memories of terribly stressful moments or episodes can be slipped into this unconscious archive for our protection. It is almost as if God were

> **"I cannot seem to get those other girls out of my mind.**
> **I would give anything to change my past."**

protecting us from an information overload by creating a place for those things that need to be laid aside for a time. Then we can process the data later, when we are healthier. Cognitive psychologists might describe it differently, but that is the general idea.

What can happen, though, is that these memories can be tapped almost randomly by sights, sound and images that somehow trigger a specific file in our unconscious mind to move to the forefront. This is what was happening to Paul. Lost images that he believed had been long forgiven and forgotten were only forgiven. In cases of sexual sin (and other traumatic life episodes that may or may not include a sexual experience), the images lie dormant until some event or sensation triggers the recovery of that experience into the conscious mind. Many therapists believe that these trapped memories can cause trouble for the mind of the client if the memories are not processed.

That's the trouble with sexual experiences. Not only is the body not ready for the trauma, the mind is not ready either. Like other areas of the body, our minds take time to mature. Putting the seemingly disconnected and random experiences of life into a reasonable order takes time. It is possible to overload the mind. We used to call this a "mental breakdown," where the confusion was so profound that memories and the ability to think become lost in the jumble.

The psychological consequences for sexually active teens are profound. Some of the psychological symptoms associated with early or risky sexual behavior include depression, suicidal thoughts, relational or disassociative disorders and eating disorders. Symptoms can also include Borderline Personality Disorder that may be characterized by anger and thoughts or feelings of undifferentiated fear and dread.

The "Add-Health" project is a nationwide survey that examines the health-related behaviors of high school students. The study has responses from over 10,000 adolescents representative of teenagers across the nation. Funded by the National Institute of Child Health and Human Development (NICHD) and 17 other federal agencies, it is the largest most significant study of its kind. And it has uncovered some troubling issues.

The psychological consequences
for sexually active teens are profound.

A full quarter of teenage girls who are sexually active report that they are depressed all, most or a lot of the time. By contrast, only 7.7 percent of teenage girls who are not sexually active report that they are depressed all, most or a lot of the time. Sexually active girls are more than three times more likely to be depressed.

More than eight percent of teenage boys who are sexually active report that they are depressed all, most or a lot of the time. Only 3.4 percent of teenage boys who are not sexually active are depressed all, most or a lot of the time. Boys who are sexually active are more than twice as likely to be depressed.

The study makes a clear link between sexual activity and attempted suicide. More than 14 percent of girls and five percent of boys who are sexually active have attempted suicide. This compares to only 5.1 percent of girls and 0.7 percent of boys who are not sexually active. Girls who are sexually active are nearly three times more likely to attempt suicide than girls who are not, and boys are eight times more likely.[1]

The trouble with these psychological imprints that come from the pain and exposure of sexual sin it that they plant lies in our mind. Lies about ourselves and others and about God. Lies like:

- If this is the only way I can be loved, then I guess I have to do this.
- Now that I have had sex, what difference does it make if I do it again?
- Who can love me now that I have crossed the line?
- God can never forgive me after what I have done.

God makes a powerful promise to those who have fallen prey to these lies. He has promised his full forgiveness, placing the sin as far away as the east is from the west. And he gives a formula of sorts for dealing with the psychological trauma of sexual sin. It is found in Paul's letter to the Ephesians:

> *You were taught, with regard to your former way of life, to put off your old self, which is being corrupted by its deceitful desires; to be made new in the attitude of your minds; and to put on the new self, created to be like God in true righteousness and holiness* (Ephesians 4:22–25).

The formula is:
Put off the old behaviors.
Be renewed in your mind.
Put on the new behaviors.

> *Therefore, I urge you, brothers, in view of God's mercy, to offer your bodies as living sacrifices, holy and pleasing to God—this is your spiritual act of worship. Do not conform any longer to the pattern of this world, but be transformed by the renewing of your mind* (Romans 12:1, 2).

This captures the critical aspect of our mind, and the role that truth plays in our recovery from sin and the trauma of sin perpetrated on us by others.

Be aware, parents, that psychological consequences of sexual behavior may not be visible. They may show up in failing grades due to an inability to concentrate, withdrawal from friends and family and signs of depression. There are lots of reasons a teen may experience any or all of these symptoms, so don't jump to the conclusion that your teen is sexually active. But the order of the day is to pay close attention to the non-verbal signs that teens display. They may be trying to tell us something very important.

EMOTIONAL CONSEQUENCES

Emotional consequences affect the heart. They may change the way we feel about life and its circumstances. No parent or youth pastor needs to be convinced that sexual activity has consequences of the heart. The feelings that go with risky sexual behavior in teens include fear, guilt, sadness, loss, shame, regret, anger, loss of self-respect and broken-heartedness. And this is just a partial list.

Nineteen million Americans suffer from depression. An estimated three million of those are teens. Dr. Meg Meeker says that is no surprise because teens are targets of a loose culture promoting promiscuity and excess. "Depression and teenagers is all about loss. It's not very complicated," Meeker said. Combine cultural pressures with existing rifts between parents and teens and you have a recipe that can spell disaster. Meeker says much of it is fueled by premarital sex. Add up the losses that teens endure: loss of virginity, loss of self-respect, loss of a sense of control over their bodies. All these things settle into their hearts and don't go anywhere.

As a physician for adolescents, Dr. Meeker treats teenagers who have become statistics of depression. She recently authored *Epidemic: How Teen Sex Is Killing Our Kids*. Meeker gives evidence to support a link between premarital sex and depression. Some teens do not agree with that assessment. One teenage boy said, "Drugs, yeah, I see how you can get depressed off that. Premarital sex, no. I think premarital sex builds character." But Meeker said, "They are told and brainwashed that sex is wonderful and sex is great, and so they go and they have these expectations, 'I'm gonna' have all these great, wonderful feelings when I have sex.' They have sex. They have all these negative feelings and they think, 'What's wrong with me? What is wrong with me?'"[2]

Thomas Lickona, a writer and educator, made this list of emotional consequences in *The Emotional Dangers of Premature Sexual Involvement.*[3]

1. Worry about pregnancy, STDs and AIDS
2. Regret
3. Guilt
4. Loss of Self-respect and self-esteem
5. Corruption of character and devaluating of sex
6. Shaken trust and fear of commitment
7. Rage over betrayal
8. Depression and suicide
9. Ruined relationships
10. Stunting personal development

The list goes on.

The invisible consequences of sin, whether they are psychological or emotional, are life-threatening. They can numb us into not caring for ourselves or others. They can confuse our minds and break our hearts. These emotional conditions often follow us into adulthood. Therapists know that there is an epidemic of bad sex in marriages for Baby Boomers who grew up in the "Sexual Revolution." The sexual "freedom" we enjoyed in our youth has come back to haunt us in our adulthood. Sexual satisfaction is tied to the health of mind and heart. When these aspects of our lives have been traumatized, sexual enjoyment can all but disappear. What a sad consequence of sin surrounding this great gift of God!

SOCIAL CONSEQUENCES

True or false? What two people do in private is nobody's business but their own.

Teens sometimes think that because some adults have privacy, they should have privacy. What they don't know is that privacy and responsibility go hand in hand. There is great responsibility in privacy. When others can see us, we are less likely to do something unwise, immoral or illegal. Shining the light on our behavior and thoughts makes us more accountable. This is a good thing! Privacy is reserved for those who have proven that they can handle the responsibility of having this protective factor removed from their lives.

When a teen becomes sexually active, all kinds of relationships are impacted. We are built to be in relationship, and any type of personal behavior, good or bad, is going to impact those around us.

The social consequences or sexual activity can be huge, and simply saying "It is none of your business" *doesn't* help. Here is what *does* help:

- As the parent or teacher, be transparent about how events in your past impacted many other people. Have ready a personal story of a significant event or situation that directly or indirectly involved important and loved people in your life. Watch for the teachable moment where it makes sense to lay this groundwork of social concern for our personal behavior. If you lay this foundation of truth early in the child's life, you can return to it again and again to refresh the idea that our behavior always impacts others we love.

- Encourage others to be a part of your teen's life. Talk to the coaches and teachers who are around your teen to be advocates for purity, self-control and self-respect. Tell grandparents and uncles and next-door neighbors that if they see a teachable moment to communicate a strong moral truth or guiding biblical principle, to go for it. Sometimes the people who will be hurt by a bad choice have never been encouraged to help our youth make good choices. Don't push those who love you away. Give them permission to

> The emotional and psychological consequences of sexual abuse and coerced sex cannot be measured. Every day thousands of children and teens are pressured into sexual encounters, many by adults in relationships of trust. The damage to the mind and heart is overwhelming. Some who have been abused cannot recover without professional care. Many abused begin to believe a complex set of lies about themselves, men (or the gender or age group that hurt them), love, God and sex. If you have a child or teen that you have reason to believe is being abused or coerced into a sexual encounter, get help immediately and get help for the child. Do not try to take on the counseling role in this person's life. Use your relationship to love, encourage and comfort.

encourage your children and teens toward good character and decisions.

- Put the protective factor of the "public eye" to work for you. Don't permit your teen to take a boyfriend or girlfriend up to a bedroom and shut the door. Don't let them be away for long periods of time alone without supervision. Trips away with the

Privacy is reserved for those who have proven

that they can handle the responsibility of having this

protective factor removed from their lives.

other's family sound innocent enough, but the value system of the other family may be different than yours. Their idea of adult supervision may be that they buy the beer for the kids so the kids don't get caught. An old Russian proverb that President Reagan used during the Cold War may seem a bit trite, but it is still true: Trust, but verify!

SPIRITUAL CONSEQUENCES

Sex plays a profound part in God's plan for human beings. The very first command recorded in the Bible that God gave to Adam and Eve was to have sexual relations (Genesis 1:28).

While the 20th century brought dramatic changes in attitudes and behaviors toward what is considered acceptable sexual behavior, the Bible is clear. Premarital and extramarital sex are sin; therefore we should avoid them completely. Why is God so adamant on this point? *To protect us from the inevitable harmful consequences, visible and invisible.* Notice Paul's warning to Christians in the sex-saturated city of Corinth:

> *Flee from sexual immorality. All other sins a man commits are out-side his body, but he who sins sexually sins against his own body* (1 Corinthians 6:18).

God created sex to be a blessing and benefit within a committed marriage. Sexual relations within the context of a loving, covenant marriage enable two people to know each other in the most intimate and personal way. Trust and belonging increase as fear and shame diminish. The couple becomes one flesh as God intended. *The International Standard Bible Encyclopedia* describes this kind of intimacy as "not just cognitive, but always experiential and deeply personal; and sexual intercourse is never just physiological, but always involves mystery and touches the whole person."[4]

All sin causes a break in our relationship with God. Our connection and intimacy with him is damaged, even destroyed. Only the forgiveness of sin through Jesus can restore us to an intimate relationship with God. But the damage does not end there. The spiritual connection between us and the Body of Christ has been harmed as well.

The mystery and differences about the opposite sex make relating to one another special. That spiritual mystery is destroyed and can be lost forever when human beings "hook up" casually. Our sexuality is a spiritual gift God gave us. We should be protect it and save it for marriage as God intended.

Any sexual experimentation outside of marriage is a mistake, for both men and women, though it does seem that women bear the brunt of the consequences. A man will never be the same in the sense that he has surrendered a sacred, spiritual part of himself that he should have reserved for his bride. Premarital sex provides momentary gratification, but it is important to count the costs: loss of purity and innocence that God intended for us. Each so-called conquest by the man robs him of some of the care and tenderness he should be cultivating for just the right woman.

Much of the attraction of sex outside of marriage is based on its illicit nature. The attitude that "stolen water is sweet, and food eaten in secret is delicious" (Proverbs 9:17) has been around for a long time. There is danger in succumbing to sexual temptation, even if getting married is your intent. When two people become "one flesh" in a sexual relationship (1 Corinthians 6:16), a spiritual bonding occurs between them. If, after they become sexually involved, one partner severs the relationship against the wishes of the other, the separation has a wrenching affect, especially for the jilted person, who is left feeling spiritually naked and ashamed. The invisible consequences all around are tremendous.

PARENTS MAKE A DIFFERENCE

Despite these unsettling invisible consequences of love gone bad, there is hope. Teenagers rate their parents as one of the biggest influencers in their decision-making process. Surveys prove it time and again. You may not believe it, but your children listen to you, even as teenagers. Parents play the most important role in combating teen depression, helping them make good choices and providing a place where they can recover from harm.

Teens battling depression and other psychological and emotional conditions related to premarital sex are often ashamed to talk with their parents. This increases their chances of finding themselves in a

Teenagers rate their parents as one of the biggest influencers in their decision-making process. Surveys prove it again and again.

deeper depression. I have heard dozens of teens say, "It would be a lot better if parents would pay more attention to kids and not act like, 'Oh well, they're teenagers, they want their space or they are going through a phase.' We need our parents in our lives."

Our teens are growing up in a world that is trying to chew them up and spit them out. What the media and popular youth entertainment business want is kids' money. The teen culture is wide open for exploitation. Unless parents get involved hard and fast, we can expect to see our children and their friends continue to suffer. Help by setting reasonable boundaries and curfews. Set boundaries on dating that are for the whole family. Communicate them clearly and be consistent in their enforcement. Usually the problem with family rules isn't the rules. It is inconsistency in enforcing them that makes a teen crazy!

A second critical difference maker is the church. Hurting teens unable to get spiritual support may try to wade through depression alone, and permanently cut spiritual ties that bind them to the church. Our goal is to build relationships of trust so that when the time of trial inevitably comes, teens have someone who can help draw them back to God and the healing only he can offer. At a time when depression in young adults is soaring, few are seeking refuge at home or in the church. Consider challenging a youth leader to offer a teen class on "Dealing with Stress" or "Helping My Friends with Depression." Make the pursuit of forgiveness and emotional healing a regular part of your prayer time. Healing doesn't stop with the physical. Seek healing from God for your teens in emotional and psychological terms. God wants to heal all of us, individually and corporately.

THE REAL DEAL ON FORGIVENESS

The answer to our fallen human condition is forgiveness. The way to healing from sexual sin is forgiveness, plain and simple. If your son or daughter has been sexually active, and perhaps depressed or suicidal, waste no time in sharing the good news of this verse:

> If we confess our sins, he is faithful and just to forgive us our sins, and to cleanse us from all unrighteousness (1 John 1:9).

John tells us that we must confess our sin—our repentance, faith and confession of sin do not accomplish forgiveness. Forgiveness comes from God through Christ. Our hearts must be reconciled to God, and reconciliation begins with confession. Help your teen understand that confession must be made in humble sincerity toward God, with faith in Christ's atoning sacrifice. You cannot mention every offence, but you dare not hide one.

Many of our teens are suffering with sin and its consequences that they are not even aware of. They need us, as caring adults, to be able to do two things well.

Speak the truth. Caring parents offer protection through their words and our deeds. We have to communicate our expectations clearly. We need to say out loud that we expect our kids to be virgins in the fullest sense of the word when they get married. We need to communicate that we do not believe in birth control as a protective factor for teens. We need to show through our own personal model that we are not controlled by the very things we do not want them to be controlled by.

Provide an environment of hope, peace, and grace where our teens can grow and make mistakes and recover. Where forgiveness is commonplace and their friends are welcome. That place is called "home."

chapter twelve

MAKE A
Difference

Her name is Kristin.

We met her several years ago when she was about to enter her senior year in high school. Over a period of several months we had made many trips to Cheyenne, and on this occasion we were there to talk with the board of directors of the local crisis pregnancy center. We were there, as senior leadership staff of Worth Waiting For, Inc., to help in the development stage of establishing a local community campaign in Cheyenne, Wyoming.

We were sitting with the board chitchatting when in walked a tall, long-haired teenager who sat down abruptly and said, "Hi, I'm Kristin." She was introduced as a high school teen who just wanted to listen to the ideas of a ministry having to do with sexual health.

We proceeded to unveil our mission and plan for a community campaign that would impact the lives of teens in Cheyenne in the area of sexual health. The adults listened, looking us in the eye and then writing notes. But Kristin just listened. She sat at the table making constant eye contact with both of us. As we were finishing our presentation, we talked about the fact that while this campaign needed an adult to lead it, the most important part of this campaign was that it was all about teen leadership in a peer-mentoring model. No one spoke. There was silence in the room and we allowed it to continue.

All of a sudden Kristin stood up.

Kristin started into a passion-filled flow of ideas that went something like this. "This is the best thing I've ever heard! My friends are dying out there. They are in constant pain—not knowing that they can be sexually pure. They are hurting each other in relationships and they think they might be pregnant—like all the time. That's why I volunteer here at the pregnancy center. I just want to help them. But this is what we need to do. We need to educate them with the truth and train them to lead others! This is awesome. Sign me up!"

Adult jaws were on the table. Everyone was speechless. Here was a high school girl, about to be a senior, who was ready to change her world.

She was fired up and ready to go and the adults knew all of the obstacles in her way. She was involved up to her eyeballs in school and church activities, sports, student government, choir; you name it, Kristin was doing it. She did not need one more thing to do.

But that was the point for Kristin. This was not one more thing to do; this was *the thing* to do.

None of the adults knew what to say. The Cheyenne campaign was at a crisis even at this early stage. Without an adult willing to step in and organize the adult prayer teams, the fundraising, the training events, the students would go unsupported and the model would fail.

Finally Angela spoke up. "I don't want to do this, but I feel God prodding me. I don't have the time, but I'm going to volunteer anyway. I'll lead the campaign if you work with me, Kristin. I'm a good organizer, but I'm rotten with teens. So you have to help me."

At the time we did not fully realize what a huge sacrifice and personal commitment this was for Angela. Angela and Fernando had four children, from teenagers down to elementary school. She was employed full time and had just taken a significant volunteer position at her local church, a new church plant. She didn't have time to do one more thing. But the Spirit of God whispered her name and she responded.

From the time these two women volunteered their time, God stepped in and unfolded the future. Kristin, a star volleyball player, quit her high school team and gave that time to the Cheyenne Worth Waiting For campaign. This was a huge sacrifice for a teen going into her senior year. Kristin gathered about eight of her friends and they began to meet as the first teen team in Cheyenne. And with Angela's help they forged ahead with almost no time to give and certainly no money.

They began to design and produce teen-led "Dessert Theaters," a collection of dramas, songs and testimonies that communicated the message of God's love and his message of purity. Hundreds of teens and parents came to their first performance.

They designed a program for high school teens to share the abstinence message with junior high students in pubic schools.

They created a Teen Covenant group, meeting twice a month to pray and encourage each other in their walk and to plan the ministry activities. Each member had signed a covenant and pledged to abstain from sexual intimacy, drugs and alcohol as long as they were a part of the Worth Waiting For Teen Team.

Then came the big dream; the goal the size of their God. Kristin and the Teen Team decided they wanted to do a Christian rock concert. They found adults to help them contact Christian rock bands in order to talk with their agents. They decided on a band and found out it would cost $20,000 to have the event. Can you imagine? They had no

Adult jaws were on the table. Everyone was speechless.

Here was a high school girl, about to be a senior,

who was ready to change her world.

money! But over the course of eight months they raised $30,000 and packed the city auditorium for a rocking concert by Third Day and Jennifer Knapp. Sitting in that auditorium and watching the sold-out concert, witnessing to over two thousand teens sign pledge cards and put them at the foot of homemade crosses was more than heart-warming. It was heavenly!

How little we expect of teenagers and how much they want to serve!

The Cheyenne Campaign is still going strong—years later. Kristin is now married and works for the Worth Waiting For campaign. Angela quit her job and worked full time on staff with Worth Waiting For, Inc. for two years. Together these two lives have changed their community and even the nation with their model of ministry.

There are now over 100 teens on Kristin's team. They still do school and church presentations among many other activities. Each teen, representing over a dozen churches in the community, is being introduced to ministry. They are being "employed," not just entertained in their faith. Their relationship is being galvanized in Christ through service, prayer and accountability. Hundreds have accepted Christ since the campaign started.

This ministry exists because, several years ago, one high school senior and one caring mom were tired of seeing teens hurt by the lies of Satan and the consequences of sexual sin.

They decided to do something about it.

We are proud to know Kristin and Angela, women of God who accepted his challenge and are changing their world, one person at a time.

What impresses you most about Kristin?

What impresses you most about Angela?

Do you believe that you could be the person to make the difference in your community? There is awesome power in one changed life. Every changed life in Christ has the full creative power of the God of the Universe dwelling inside. We live day by day with the power, but not daily using the power. What a cosmic shame! We forget and believe the lie that even though we are Christians, we are essentially the same as those who are not. That is not true. Christians are indwelled with the

Spirit and we have a purpose above all purposes!

Here is the truth that Kristin and Angela knew that released the Power of the Holy Spirit in their lives:

Therefore, if anyone is in Christ, he is a new creation; the old has gone, the new has come! All this is from God, who reconciled us to himself through Christ and gave us the ministry of reconciliation: that God was reconciling the world to himself in Christ, not counting men's sins against them. And he has committed to us the message of reconciliation. We are therefore Christ's ambassadors, as though God were making his appeal through us. We implore you on Christ's behalf: Be reconciled to God. God made him who had no sin to be sin for us, so that in him we might become the righteousness of God (2 Corinthians 5:17–21).

This passage tells us that we have a Task, a Title and a Testimony.

Our **Task** is to be ministers of reconciliation. That means that we confront lies with the truth and invite—this passage says implore or beg—others to live in peace with God; to lay aside the lies of sin to accept the forgiveness and healing of God. Healing for every sexual sin and sadness you can imagine.

God has given us a **Title**, too: Ambassador. We do not live here; our home is heaven and the laws we live by are the laws of heaven. We represent our king on this soil, convincing those of this land of the good will of our heavenly king.

And we have a **Testimony**. If our task is reconciliation and our Title ambassador, we'd better have a clear story to tell. And this is our story:

God made him who had no sin to be sin for us, so that in him we might become the righteousness of God (2 Corinthians 5:21).

Our testimony is that all our sin and sadness has been paid for and we no longer have to pay attention to the lies, to be held hostage to the deception. And neither do the ones we love. Kristin and Angela released the power of God in them. You can, too. We dare you!

At the beginning of this book, we challenged you to decide to talk to your kids about sexuality. That decision is the first step in helping them know God's truth about love, sex and relationships. But keeping that commitment is not a one-time thing. It's a relationship. You can give your kids all the facts for them to store in their heads. The values you want to put in their hearts may take a little longer. If you're a parent, you're permanently on call!

How did you feel about talking to your kids about sexuality at the beginning of this book?

How do you feel about it now?

What has made the difference?

Your job starts with your own kids. That's probably why you picked up this book in the first place. You're striving to model the love of God to your kids, whatever age they are, so that they will learn to love and follow him.

But not too many families live on an island all by themselves. Your kids, especially teenagers, are part of a culture and community. They play on teams, they go to school, they watch movies, they attend youth group meetings, they flip through magazines, they may even have jobs. They see and talk to other kids and adults all the time. Magazines, television, movies, music—it's all part of the culture they're growing up in.

So maybe, just maybe, your job goes beyond your family's borders to the family next door or down the street or across the church. While parents are the single greatest influence on their kids' lives, they don't have to feel alone. Kids of all ages respond to significant adults in their lives who are not their parents. Your son may be grunting and shrugging his shoulders at you, but his friend seems to babble incessantly every time he's in your house. Your daughter may find a friend in the mom next door.

Talk to the parents of your kids' friends. Sift out the ones you trust. Form an alliance of sorts, pledging to help each other's kids through tough spots with honest answers. Be a positive voice in the life of a child or teenager who is not yours but needs you very much.

Be the culture that you want your kids to learn. With the support of other parents, create a culture of honest questions and answers, of truth, of unconditional love, of support and affirmation for standing

Kids of all ages respond to significant adults

in their lives who are not their parents.

up for what's right and not giving in to the moment. If you're studying this book with a group, you've shared with each other for several weeks. You're on your way to a support group. If you're studying this book alone, share it with a few other parents who undoubtedly have many of the same questions and struggles that you have.

Kristin and Angela changed the culture. They embraced the Task, the Title and the Testimony, not only for themselves, but for teens all over the city of Cheyenne.

What will you do?

LEADER'S GUIDE

CHAPTER 1
It's Time to Talk
Step 1: On the Same Page

Summarize the chapter with the following information.

Talking with our kids about sex makes a lot of us nervous. We don't know what to say or when to say it. And we're not sure they're even listening anyway. Part of why it's awkward is because many of our parents didn't talk to us. Somehow we got the idea that it's not okay to talk about these subjects, and sometimes we pass that attitude on to our kids.

Jesus used a mentoring model with the people he wanted to influence. He gathered the disciples around him, and they went everywhere with him. Wherever he went, they followed. It was all about being with Jesus. And the result was people who were radically changed and committed to spreading the message that Jesus came to bring.

Pause here to read Acts 4:1–13.

- How did being with Jesus impact Peter and John?
- How does being with Jesus impact us?
- How does our being with Jesus impact our kids?

We have more of an influence on our kids than we think. They're watching us and learning from our models. It's up to us to model godly behavior that we want them to learn, and to be ready and alert for those times when our kids want to have a conversation. Let's explore some ideas that will make us more comfortable talking to our kids about sex.

Step 2: What Did We Learn?

- What key idea from this chapter stands out to you the most? Why?
- What one word describes what your parents discussed with you about sex, love and relationships? What one word describes how you felt during that discussion?

- When your kids are grown, what feelings would you like them to have about how you handled sex, love and relationships?

- How would you describe a teachable moment? How would you recognize a teachable moment in your child?

Step 3: Prayer and Dare

Close your time together by praying for each other and asking for God's guidance. Pray a prayer like this one.

God, it's easy for us to shy away from the task of talking to our kids about sexuality. We think we don't have to do it today, there's plenty of time, and then the time gets away from us. We ask for your courage to talk to our kids about these important subjects. Give us the wisdom to recognize teachable moments and to use them with love and sensitivity. Help us to support each other and pray for each other. In Jesus' name, amen.

Dare for the Week:

Consider starting a mentoring relationship or being in a mentoring relationship with a young person in your church. Call your church leadership and see if they have a mentoring or discipleship program. If they don't have one, suggest starting one. See if the youth leaders need help encouraging some particular teens in their group.

CHAPTER 2
The Battle at Your Doorstep
Step 1: On the Same Page

Summarize the chapter with the following information.

One of the main reasons that we have failed to win the war for our young people is that we have believed lies ourselves. We feel like we are not qualified to talk about sex, love and relationships because of our failings in the past. We even sin against our kids and don't want to admit it and ask forgiveness. We believe lies that Satan is telling us about ourselves. So instead of confronting those lies, we lose the war of truth before it even starts.

Not only have we felt disqualified, but some of us feel like our time has passed. We feel that our teens don't listen to us anymore and they don't respect us. We feel that we have lost our position to influence. We need hints on how to rebuild relationships and how to get reinserted into our teen's life.

Pause here to read Ephesians 6:10–12 aloud.

- How does this passage apply to talking to our kids about sexuality?
- What is the biggest spiritual obstacle that gets in our way of talking to our kids?

We need to turn up the heat when it comes to modeling, especially for our older teens. They need to see us work in the fulcrum of life, when the times are hard. We often find it hard to admit our mistakes and doubts and fears. Sometimes there are the parts of us that our older teens need to see. We want our kids to see that we need each other in the family and that God is satisfying our most personal fears and doubts.

Step 2: What Did We Learn?

- Why is forgiveness for what we've done in the past important for how we help our kids learn about sex, love and forgiveness?
- If we believe that God forgives us, why is it so hard to forgive ourselves and move on with confidence that we are new creations?
- Is it too late to make an impact on your kids in the areas of sex, love and relationships? Why or why not?
- On a scale of 1 to 10, how consistent are you in modeling the behaviors you want your kids to learn? What can you do to become more consistent?
- What Bible verses can you think of that might encourage others in the group to turn away from Satan's lies and believe in God's truth?

Step 3: Prayer and Dare

Close your session with a time of prayer. Challenge group members to take seriously the call to join the Fellowship of the King. Ask them to stand or kneel to present themselves physically to God. Pray a prayer like this one:

> *Dear God, the evil one has been lying to us. Sometimes we believe we are disqualified because of our past sin or even current sins. That is a lie. You have forgiven all of our sin and you call us your own. We are children of the king. Forgive us for our times of unbelief.*
>
> *Satan tempts us to believe that it is too late or we are too old or our children are no longer listening. Sometimes it's easier to settle in front of the TV than to read that book we should read or memorize Scripture that would comfort us in times of stress. Remind us in to pay more attention to your workings in our spirits.*
>
> *Father, right now, you want us for service. Now in the quietness of our spirits we listen for you to say our names even as you called out to Samuel and Moses and Paul. We lift our hands as a symbol of humbleness. Use us to give our kids a picture of what it means to live for you. Help us to model ourselves after you and make choices that honor you. Help us to believe your truth. In Jesus' name, amen.*

Dare for the Week:

Share what God has said to you today with someone who is not here now and will understand and encourage you. Take time and reflect with the person out loud. See if the person you share with will ask penetrating questions that take you even deeper into your thoughts and resolve. See if this person will pray for you for the next 10 days, as Satan will do his best to try to come and snatch up this seed before it has a chance to root well. Enlist someone to watch your backside in prayer.

CHAPTER 3
Kids in Context
Step 1: On the Same Page
Summarize the chapter with the following information.

Sociologists are having a tough time agreeing on a label for this generation of teens. A lot like Generation Y. Some prefer Millenialists. We've even heard Echo Boomers. Some call them Gen N or Gen Net. Whatever sociologists call them, most teens them don't like the label.

Encompassing more than 70 million people born between 1980 and 1996, Millenialists are, at their core, the largest group of teenagers in American history. This generation dwarfs even its parent's generation, the Baby Boomers, who came of age in the 1960s. In the next decade, this generation will come to represent 41 percent of the U.S. population, according to the Census Bureau.

If we're going to be able to talk to this generation, we have to understand the context they're growing up in. The results of questionnaires show modern-day young people are an optimistic, stress-driven, team-oriented and a multitasking generation. They are more conservative than their brothers and sisters 10 years older, yet they are more active and tend to volunteer more. Like most young people, they still spend an incredible amount of money ($275 billion spent annually, according to some estimates!). Many believe that the events of September 11, 2001 will have a profound impact on the conscience and soul of this generation as this young culture was the first to ever see a terrorist attack on our own soil.

And as hard as they are to label, they are even harder to quantify. There are multiple sub-cultures, as evidenced by their music and the lack of one headlining star. There are more first, second and third generations of immigrants from Asia and Mexico who have lost many of the most significant aspects of their grandparents' culture.

Changing sexual behaviors seem to be the one aspect they all have in common. They are the first generation that has, for their lifetime, lived with sex education in schools, HIV, condoms available for the asking and abortion without parental approval. They have been presented "safe sex" and "abstinence education." They are making significant choices and we would be well advised to pay attention to their decisions.

We'd better pay attention to their decisions because one day they will be taking care of us in our old age!

Step 2: What Did We Learn?

According to Dr. Scott Stanley of the University of Denver:

- Approximately 31% of your friends and co-workers, aged 35 to 54, who are married, engaged or cohabitating have already been previously divorced.

- If your parents have been married many years (let's say 35+ years) and have never been divorced, the likelihood of their marriage ending in divorce is nil.

- A young couple marrying for the first time today has a lifetime divorce risk of 40%, unless current trends change significantly.

The good news is the rate of divorces per year per 1000 people in the U.S. has been declining since 1981. Today there are at their lowest since 1972, over 30 years. *Source: www.smartmarriages.com/divorcestats.html.*

- What do you think are the implications of growing up within a culture of divorce?

- Divorce has become a difficult dynamic for the church. We want to be a place of healing, but so often the divorced feel condemned and judged at their local church fellowship? Have you experienced this for you or your friends and what do you think we can do to develop a spirit of grace, forgiveness and healing?

- How do you react to the information on the TimeLine? Do you feel that teens have always had a tough time adjusting to growing up or is their world really more stressful? What other major considerations would you add to the Millenialist TimeLine?

- How do you feel about the fact that Christians teens are not significantly different in their sexual behaviors than non-Christians?

Step 3: Prayer and Dare

Close your session with a prayer like this one:

Dear God, we ask you today to protect our teens from the sadness and brokenness of the world that seeks to overpower them. Put a hedge of protection around them and send angels to cover their paths. They have pressures and temptations that I never had to face as a teen. We pray that you would protect them and prepare them to be mighty servants of your kingdom. Give us courage to pay attention to their victories and struggles. We pray that you would protect them specifically from sexual sin and the consequences that go with those temptations. In Jesus name, amen.

Dares for the Week:

1. Call or visit your youth pastor or a volunteer youth worker at your church. Ask about the culture of the church, what kind of things it seems that the church youth group is going through. Ask if there have there been any issues for the teens that you can pray about. Avoid asking about your own teen; instead, focus on the group as a whole.

2. Ask your youth pastor or volunteer youth worker specifically what he or she is going through as a youth worker. The pressures to be a model to so many teens and to keep up with the schedule of life in such a pressure packed dynamic as youth ministry is intense. Offer to pray for your youth worker right then, in person or on the phone. Show to yourself and to the pastor and volunteers and to God that you mean business about getting involved in every way that makes sense in the lives of your teens.

CHAPTER 4
Sex Education: The Surprising Facts
Step 1: On the Same Page

Summarize the chapter with the following information.

We live in a world of lies. Dangerous lies spun by the author of lies. Some of these lies have been told to our children regarding their sexuality. Our job as parents, teachers and adult caregivers in a position of trust is to tell the truth. When our children believe lies about sex, it could kill them.

Alfred Kinsey started some terrible lies back in the 1950s. His flawed studies stated some hard-to-believe conclusions, like "We are sexual from birth," opening the door to sex at any age. The Sex Information and Education Council of the United States (SIECUS) built upon those lies, encouraging homosexuality as an equally acceptable lifestyle and teaching third graders about masturbation. SIECUS sex education guidelines have been the backbone of our public school sex education system in the U.S. for the past 40 years.

Recently a movement toward abstinence education has risen, returning to traditional family values of purity, delayed gratification and the importance of marriage to provide an environment of safety and trust for sex. "Abstinence Only" education emphasizes a parent's role in sex education and prioritizes character development, not condom education.

Character-based sex education, the basis for abstinence education, is the best the world can offer. But Christian parents can offer Christ-centered sex education in the homes, churches and Christian schools. Christ-centered sex education focuses on motives and attitudes, not just outward behavior. Christ-centered education makes sex everything God intended it to be.

Step 2: What Did We Learn?

- Do you think that it is harder to be a teenager in this day than it was for us as teens?

Erik Erickson, who some consider to be the "Father of Developmental Psychology," describes our lives as having several stages of growth. One of these stages happens between the age of six to 12 and is called the Industry or Latency Period. During this stage we are capable of learning, creating and accomplishing numerous new skills and knowledge, thus developing a sense of industry. Sexual feelings are appropriately dormant or latent during this time, with healthy individuals being more interested in same gender friendship of a non-sexual nature. He also states that this is also a very social stage of development and if we experience unresolved feelings of inadequacy and inferiority among our peers, we can have serious problems in terms of competence and self-esteem.

As the world expands a bit, our most significant relationship is with the school and neighborhood. Parents are no longer the complete authorities they once were, although they are still important.

- Do you think that there is a general period of latency or innocence in children of grade school age when it comes to sexual feelings and behavior?
- What do you think is a normal time for sexual feelings to develop?
- What do you think are the short- and long-term consequences of the fact that our young children are being exposed to explicit sexual images on the TV and in the movies during this latency period?
- How can we help to keep this period for our children innocent?

Step 3: Prayer and Dare

Close your session with a prayer like this one:

Dear God, we see that people who don't know you and follow your way are not telling the truth to our kids. They don't have your picture of how a child develops, yet they have great influence in schools. We ask that you give our school superintendents and principles and teachers great wisdom. Give courage and strength to the Christian teachers on our public school campuses.

Thank you for ministries and organizations that are fighting to bring to truth to our school and churches about the kinds of lies being spread to our teens regarding sexual health and purity. We pray for our church and for those of us in this group. Give us courage, for we see how great a challenge there is for the lives of our children. Help us to make a difference. In Jesus' name, amen.

Dare for the Week:

1. Visit web sites for the following groups and see the difference in how they approach important concepts such as when a teen should be encouraged to experiment with sex and what kind of roles parents are to play in sex education. Be prepared to share with your group the next time you meet.

Planned Parenthood

SIECUS

Medical Institute for Sexual Health

National Abstinence Clearinghouse

Worth Waiting For, Inc.

Heartbeat International

2. Call your school and find out when they begin sex education and what kinds of materials they cover. Ask if they have the Medical Institute for Sexual Health guidelines for sex education. If they don't, offer to provide a copy.

3. Sit down with your children or teens and ask them when they began to have sex education. If they go to a private Christian school, ask them if they know who sets the standards for sex education on their campus. See if they think the issues of teen sexuality are being handled openly and with truth on their campus. Start considering what you might be able to do on their campus to help.

CHAPTER 5
Confront the Lies
Step 1: On the Same Page

Summarize the chapter with the following information.

We live in a world of lies. Unfortunately, our kids may not always know the difference between the truth and a lie. When it comes to sexuality and the choices they make, believing the lies can be devastating. Eight lies that teens hear about sex are:

Sex is bad.

Sex is love and love is sex.

Sex is an obligation.

It's all my fault.

It only affects the two of us.

I won't get pregnant.

I won't get a disease.

I won't get AIDS.

Our job as parents is to challenge these lies and help our kids see God's truth instead. We can look at the Bible to see what God's says about sex, love and relationships. We can focus on some parenting basics:

- Be a parent first, not a friend first.
- Be in their world.
- Be just, not fair.
- Communicate clearly.
- Help them succeed.
- Trust is earned. Love is given.

Step 2: What Did We Learn?

Look up each of these Bible verses together and talk about what you can learn about sex from each verse. You might like to ask group members to put each verse in their own words.

> Genesis 2:25: *Adam and Eve were naked and not ashamed.*
>
> Song of Solomon 5:1; 6:3, 8: *The beauty and passion of sex.*
>
> Matthew 19:6: *Jesus honors covenant marriage.*
>
> Ephesians 5:21–32: *Marriage and the character of God.*
>
> 1 Corinthians 7:3: *Sex is an expected part of a fulfilling marriage.*

- What difference does the truth about sex make in people's lives?
- What price will our kids pay if we don't make sure they know the truth?

Step 3: Prayer and Dare

Close your time together with a pray like this one.

> *Dear God, we praise you for your plan for the family. From the very beginning you designed marriage and family. You designed it so that children would be our blessing and that becoming one flesh was our gift of intimacy from you.*
>
> *Because we find it difficult or embarrassing, we avoid the conversations about sexual intimacy. We ask you to move today in the lives of our teens. Help us help them challenge the lies they hear around them and decide to honor you.*

We especially pray for the teens who have been traumatized by abuse and have experienced sexual coercion. We pray for these unseen wounds of the mind and heart and that you would heal those hurt in this way.

Be with all your families here and give us courage to do the right things and to be salt and light in our community and work place.

In Jesus' name, amen.

Dares for the Week:

1. Take one of the six basic parenting bullet points (pages 82–84) and talk about that dynamic in your home. Talk with your spouse and with one of your teenage children. Be sure to listen as well as talk. Seek to understand what other members of your family are thinking and feeling about your house rules.

2. Pray about being in a mentoring relationship with someone in your church. Call your church leadership and see if they have a mentoring or discipleship program. If they don't have one, consider starting one. See if the youth leaders need help encouraging some particular teens in their group.

CHAPTER 6
Marriage: Beautiful by Design
Step 1: On the Same Page

Summarize the chapter with the following information.

Kids today are growing up with all kinds of ideas about marriage, and many of these ideas are contrary to God's design for marriage. God created marriage. It was all his idea in the first place! The marriage relationship is the perfect place to express the gift of sexuality that God has given us. To teach our kids about sexuality in marriage, we have to know what God's Word says. And then we have to model what we say we believe, because our kids are watching and learning from us how to be married. Are they learning what we want them to learn?

Genesis 2:18–25 tells us about the very first marriage. From this story, we can learn that God means marriage to be:

- monogamous
- heterosexual
- separate and permanent
- intimate

Ephesians 5:22–33 is a key New Testament passage about marriage. Paul talks about the relationship between Christ and the church as a picture of the relationship between husband and wife. Key points Paul makes about marriage are:

- unity in the relationship
- acting with sacrificial love
- headship and submission in the image of Christ
- taking delight in each other.

Step 2: What Did We Learn?

- How did your early expectations for marriage differ from reality once you were married?
- What do you wish you had known about marriage before you got married?
- Some people see marriage and sex as two separate ideas that might come together for some people, but not necessarily. Why is it important to help our kids see marriage and sex as a whole package that is worth waiting for?
- What Bible passages about marriage would you like to challenge your teens to study?

Step 3: Prayer and Dare

Close your time together with a prayer like this one.

Lord, thank you for creating us as sexual beings. And thank you for giving us marriage as a safe and trusting place for us to express our sexuality. We fail, Lord. Every day, we miss opportunities for sacrificial love. Other times we see the opportunity and we just don't want to make the sacrifice. Remind us that our kids are watching. They see when we turn away from helping a spouse, or when we speak a harsh word. Help us to be more consistent, positive models of a love rela-

*tionship. Give us the courage to talk with our kids about this impor-
tant subject. And may our actions be consistent with what we say. In
Jesus' name, amen.*

Dare for the Week:

Make a goal to be consciously more thoughtful about the love
relationship you're modeling with your spouse in front of your kids.
Think of one new action a day that shows a self-sacrificing attitude
toward your spouse. Make sure that some of these actions are things
your kids can observe. Other ideas will be appropriate for the privacy
of your bedroom, and your kids will see the natural outflow that comes
from a strengthened relationship between their parents.

CHAPTER 7
Questions and Answers
Step 1: On the Same Page
Summarize the chapter with the following information.

Parents have a lot of questions about how to approach the subject of
sexuality. First we have to get past our own discomfort and
embarrassment. We need to think about what situations might come
up and how we should respond. Some things might never happen, but
it's better to have thought about them ahead of time than to be
surprised when they do come up. This session will give us a chance to
talk about things like consequences for unacceptable behaviors, setting
boundaries, rebuilding trust when it has been broken, and how to talk
to a teen who has been sexually active. It's our job as parents to help
our kids know God's truth and not be sucked into the relativism they
see and hear all around them.

Step 2: What Did We Learn?
- Which of the questions in this chapter do you identify with the
  most? Why?
- Why is it important to be consistent about rules and
  consequences?
- If you had to give one guideline for setting boundaries for
  sexual behavior, what would it be?

- How much do you think your kids know about the consequences of sexual behavior? Do they know enough to make sound decisions?
- What do you think are the best places to get answers and advice on questions about sexuality?
- How can parents support each other in the task of teaching healthy God-honoring sexuality to their kids?

Step 3: Prayer and Dare

Close your session with a prayer like this one:

> *Dear God, we ask you today to search our minds and see if there is any falsehood or lie in us. Have we so slipped in our own thinking that we cannot see the lie for the truth? We want to be able to model the truth for our children, for the children in my care. You are Truth. Help us to find a way this week to test and see if our children believe the lie that all ways are as good as any other. Help us face questions that we think won't happen to us. Prepare us for the teachable moments that you have in store for our children, so we will be ready with your truth. Help us to support each other as parents in the task of caring for the children you have given us. In Jesus name, amen.*

Dares for the Week:

1. For an academic review of Christianity and the post-modern thought debate check out "Orthodoxy in Post-Modern Pluralistic Societies" by Fr. Thomas Hook. Find it at OrthodoxyToday.org. It is part of a series called "Commentary on Social and Moral Issues of the Day." The URL is http://www.orthodoxytoday.org/articles/HopPMod.htm.

2. Ask your teen three research questions without getting into a debate or trying to change their mind. Just ask the question, get your answer and say "Thanks, I was just curious what you thought."

Question 1: Do you believe that sex is a private issue and that anything between two people is their own business, or do you believe that there should be some restraints on sex? How come?

Question 2: Do you think that 18 year old can date responsibly? How about 16 year olds? 12 year olds? Six year olds?

Question 3: What is responsible dating?

3. Go to the library or buy a copy of *FEM* or *Cosmopolitan* and look through it for lies. Share those lies with your spouse or a friend, or bring them back to the group next week.

CHAPTER 8
Intimacy and Boundaries
Step 1: On the Same Page

Summarize the chapter with the following information.

All of us to who call Jesus Christ Savior want to live lives that honor and respect him. But too often we fail. The Apostle Paul himself lamented, "The very things I want to do I do not do and the things I do, I do not want to do. Who will save me from this?" (Romans 7:14). Throughout Christian history, sexual sin has claimed some of the finest, most dedicated leaders. Learning to control our desires, especially our sexual desires, is part of what it means to be a mature Christian.

Controlling sexual desires is not so much about striving and straining against sin as it is about yielding to God. It means understanding the nature of intimacy. Physical intimacy starts innocently as showing affection, then romance, then sexual satisfaction. The self-controlled person sets boundaries as these steps of intimacy deepen, and the more specific the boundaries the better the chance of success. And intimacy is much more than just sex. Much more!

Boundaries mean knowing ourselves, because one person's simple kiss is another person's sexual unleashing. Helping another person to set boundaries is tricky business. It is especially difficult for parents of teens, as our teens pull away from us and listen less and watch us more. Still we need to help our teens understand God's non-negotiables and how to apply his advice to flee immorality. We have to talk about it all the time and communicate in no uncertain terms what we expect out of our children.

We want to leave our teens a legacy, so we have to teach them what it looks like and how to get there. Refusal skills are taught and caught. As parents and teachers, we have to teach them how to say no and mean it. And we have to show them that mature Christian adults do this all the time, because often values are caught not taught.

Step 2: What Did We Learn?

- Suggest three other words that you could use to convey to meaning of "intimacy" to your kids.
- True intimacy is about being fully known as a whole person. On a scale of 1 to 10, how intimate a relationship do you have with your kids? Explain.
- Why is it important to have an intimate relationship with God before having an intimate relationship with another person?
- What do you think keeps kids from understanding what real intimacy is? How can we help our kids get around those obstacles?
- What boundaries does your family have for dating? Do you have rules about the age for dating or what kids can do on a date, or curfews for a date? How well do you think the boundaries are working?

Step 3: Prayer and Dare

Close your time together with a prayer like this one:

> *Dear God, we want to be intimate with you. Our lives with you are the most important relationship we have, but sometimes we let the things of this world distract us. And we confess that the disciplines of the Spirit which can bring us close to you are hard for us. Prayer, study, worship, confession, fasting. All of these take a special commitment. Help us to commit here that we will seek you and your holiness with more purpose this week. If we want our kids to know that abiding in you is the basis for all intimacy, then we must abide in you ourselves.*

> *Father, we pray that our teens will be able to apply good boundaries to their dating lives. Help them to develop self-respect, self-restraint and self-control. Show us the teachable moments and give us just the*

right words to say for each occasion.

We pray that our families and marriages would be known for their love and intimacy. Help us to not settle for second best, busy lives of being together. Instead let our families and this church be beacons of caring and intimacy and health. In Jesus' name, amen.

Dare for the Week:

If you are married, use the Intimacy Inventory for Married Partners (page 129) to reflect on how you are doing at developing intimacy in your relationship. Consider taking a specific time to pray with your spouse for your marriage, that it would be more intimate and sacrificial.

If you are single, think about your relationship with your children and extended family. What could be keeping them from being more intimate?

Take your teen out for lunch and take 15 minutes to have him or her skim this chapter. Then ask two questions.

1. "Just looking at this chapter quickly, what one thing do you see in this book that you think you agree with. Why?"

2. "Again just skimming this chapter, what one thing here do you think you disagree with? Why?"

Don't try to talk your teen out of his or her opinion. Just listen and then say thanks for helping you to understand this issue.

CHAPTER 9
Hot Topics
Step 1: On the Same Page

Summarize the chapter with the following information.

Every family needs to face the difficult issues of sexual behavior and to take a stand, coming to a place of resolve based on the firm foundation of God's word.

This chapter covered hot topics of the world of sexual behavior and sin: living together, pornography and masturbation, abortion and contraception and homosexuality. If we are going to confront lies and teach the truth to our kids, we have to be ready to give a firm defense of our stand. To do that, we have to understand God's stand. As we read, we looked at some Bible verses to find out what God's Word says and what it doesn't say. We also read some statistics about reality. We may think these things won't happen to our kids, raised in good Christian families, but they might. Our strongest defense is to be proactive and be ready for teachable moments. We don't have to give a lecture on each topic. But we do need to be ready for candid conversation when the opportunities arise.

Step 2: What Did We Learn?

- What's the first thing that goes through your head when one of your kids brings up one of these controversial topics? What do you feel in your heart at those times?
- What do you think is the risk that one of your kids would decide to move in with a boyfriend or girlfriend? What would you say if that happened?

Break into small groups and have each group talk about one of these situations, then share what each group has discussed with the large group.

You've just discovered that your 14-year-old son has logged onto several pornographic sites. What will you say to him?

Your 16-year-old daughter wants to go to school without a bra. What will you say to her?

A friend at church says that issues of sexuality, including homosexuality and cohabitating, are personal and none of the church's business. What do you say?

Step 3: Prayer and Dare

Close your session with a prayer like this one.

Father, we admit that there are many things we would prefer to not talk about. We get embarrassed and afraid we'll make a mistake and hurt someone or look foolish. Father, we ask you for courage and resolve. It's so easy to turn our heads and just secretly hope these things won't happen to our kids so we don't have to deal with them. We ask your protection for our kids, and we ask for your Spirit to guide our conversations with them as we help them understand your truth on these hot topics. Help us not to shrink away from opportunities, from teachable moments, but rather to step right up and say what needs to be said. In Jesus' name, amen.

Dare for the Week:

As a small group or class, discuss which of these hot topics your church could better address. Come up with two or three programs or interventions that your church could do to address these needs. Take your ideas to the governing body of your church, offering to help as God leads them to proceed.

CHAPTER 10
Handling Teen Pregnancy and Disease
Step 1: On the Same Page

Summarize the chapter with the following information.

In this session we're looking at the visible, physical consequences of sex. Teen pregnancy affects a wide circle of people around the youth and changes life forever. Disease can haunt an individual for a lifetime.

We can help our kids make good sexual choices by talking about God's plan for sexuality and being candid with information. This chapter presents key information about diseases that we can use to talk with our kids. We can be a source of information that they can trust, and we'll have the satisfaction of knowing that they know the real facts. But even with all these safeguards, some kids will make choices that have physical consequences. Some teenagers will find themselves pregnant or infected with a disease. If that happens, we can better help them through the process if we understand the facts ourselves.

Step 2: What Did We Learn?

Break up into groups of two or three and discusses your thoughts and feelings for the following questions:

How would you feel if your daughter came home and said, "I'm pregnant"?

What would be the first thing out of your mouth if your son came home and said, "My girlfriend is pregnant and it's my baby"?

- Look at the facts about teen pregnancy beginning on page 148. Do any of these surprise you? Why or why not?
- Read Psalm 139:13–16 aloud together. Discuss the ideas from these verses that you want your children to understand. What can you do to teach these ideas at home?
- What do you think is the most important thing parents can do to help teens make choices that avoid pregnancy and STDs?
- How much do you think your kids know about STDs? Is it enough? Explain.
- If your son or daughter faced pregnancy or an STD, what would be the most important thing you could do to help in that situation?

Step 3: Prayer and Dare

Close your session with a prayer like this one.

> *God, we come to you in humbleness and repentance. We confess our temptation to forget others who are suffering the consequences of sexual choices. We even think, "It won't happen in my family." Lord, teach us how to respond to the need of others facing pregnancy and disease.*
>
> *For our children, Father, we ask for your grace and healing. Protect those we love from the ravages of sexually transmitted disease. We pray for a revival of purity among our young people and that the teens at our church would be swept up in the holiness of God so that they would become the strong lights of truth in their world and among their friends. Give them courage to help their friends who find themselves in trouble. In Jesus' name, amen.*

Dares for the Week:

1. Do an Internet search on "sexually transmitted disease" or one of the specific diseases discussed in this chapter and see what kind of sites

are out there to explore. Look at several. See if the facts are the same from site to site. Make a note of the sites that you think are the best and share those with your group next week.

2. Call your family doctor or OB/GYN and see what his or her opinion is on talking to their patients about sexually transmitted disease and the use of condoms and whether they promote abstinence until marriage. Be prepared to offer your opinion.

3. Contact your church missions department and see what they are doing to support AIDS work internationally.

4. Call or visit a local Christian crisis pregnancy center and ask how you can volunteer. Invite your teen to go with you.

CHAPTER 11
Consequences and Healing
Step 1: On the Same Page
Summarize the chapter with the following information.

Most teens live in the present moment and don't think a lot about the future consequences of choices that they make now. But their choices in the area of sexual health can have far-reaching consequences, and we need to help them understand the psychological, emotional, social and spiritual consequences that may follow them for years. Sexually active teens are at a far higher risk of depression and suicide than teens who are not sexually active. But this is an invisible indicator. Parents may not recognize the signs or be unaware of the roots of the problem.

Contrary to what we think, teenagers do listen to their parents. As long as we're willing to talk candidly, we can be the greatest influence in our kids' lives on this issue. We can help prevent the invisible consequences of early sexual behavior. For teens who have already become sexually active, we can offer the grace of God's forgiveness and a clean start.

Step 2: What Did We Learn?
Do this activity with your whole group.

Imagine that your son or daughter has made a pledge to be sexually pure before marriage. Now imagine that he or she has broken this pledge and been sexually active. Now your daughter or your son's girlfriend is pregnant.

Go through the following list of friends and family and write down on a white board or flip chart how that new circumstance changes the lives of your child's social environment:

The mom	Past boyfriends or girlfriends
The dad	Current best friend
The grandparents	People at church
The coaches	Younger brothers and sisters

- What do you think about the idea that although the mental images of previous sexual relationships may never truly go away, they can lose their power over us?

Dr. Meg Meeker, in her book *How Teen Sex is Killing our Kids,* said, "Every parent needs to realize that they have tremendous power in their kids' lives. Go after your kids. Don't be afraid of your kids. Your kids want you to come after them, pursue them. If you are afraid that your teenager is out on a date sleeping with a guy, find out where she is and show up." Reclaiming a strong connection between parent and child is key.

- Why do you think it is so hard for parents to talk to their own teens about sexuality?
- Many parent and adults fear teenagers. Why is that?
- What one or two specific things do you think you could do to improve the relationship you have with your teens?
- Which of the four invisible consequences of sex (psychological, emotional, social and spiritual) do you think has the longest lasting impact? Why?

Step 3: Prayer and Dare

Close your time together with a prayer like this one.

Dear God, I ask you today to make us instruments of your healing. We want to be a part of healing the invisible hurt of others. The con-

sequence of sin is so real and so terrible. We treasure your forgive-
ness once and for all. Help us to be salt and light in the lives of our
children and to their friends. Protect our children from the lies of this
world, especially the lies of the evil one who would trap them in sex-
ual sin. I ask for your protection and care for these innocent ones I
love so much. In Jesus' name, amen.

Dares for the Week:

Go to the school where your children attend and, after clearing it with
the office, walk the halls for several minutes. Plan it so that you can be
there during the changing of classes or during lunch. Note the
temptations and pressures that are before them all the time. Be
prepared to talk about what you have discovered with your class or
small group.

CHAPTER 12
Make a Difference
Step 1: On the Same Page
Summarize the chapter by retelling the story of Kristin and Angela
from pages 185–188.

Step 2: What Did We Learn?
- What's the biggest difference in how you feel about talking
  about sexuality from the beginning of the book to the end?
- Share a verse or passage that has given you encouragement in
  this process.
- What are some practical things you want to be sure you do as
  a result of studying this book?
- How can we continue to support each other in the parenting
  task now that we have finished this book?

Step 3: Prayer and Dare
Close your time with a prayer like this one.

Father, thank you for people like Kristin and Angela. Thank you for
the example of their lives. Thank you for your Spirit working in them.

Thank you for the commitment they made to "see it through" even though they had plenty of good reasons not to. Remind us that we do not have to do everything in our own strength, but that you give us the strength and encouragement to carry out the work that you call us to. You've given us children and the job of bringing them to love and honor you. Help us to do just that as we talk in future week and months and years about sexuality with our kids. And if you have a greater vision for us, help us not to close our eyes but to see just what you want us to do for each other and for each other's kids and for other kids in our community. Lead us, Lord, because we want to follow you. In Jesus' name, amen.

Dare for the Week:

Share what you've learned from reading this book with three other parents this week. Use your experience to open up channels of support with other parents you know.

NOTES

Chapter 3 Kids in Context

1. "TV Sex, Violence Triples," *TV & Entertainment*, May 2000.
2. *Sexual Health Knowledge, Attitudes and Experiences* (Menlo Park, CA: The Henry J. Kaiser Family Foundation, 2003).
3. "Teenagers." Barna Research Online (2003). www.barna.org
4. Op Cit. Kaiser study.

Chapter 4 Sex Education: The Surprising Facts

1. James H. Jones, *Alfred C. Kinsey: A Public/Private Life* (New York: W.W. Norton & Company, 1997), 4.
2. "Harming the Little Ones: The Effects of Pedophilia on Children," Family Research Council. www.frc.org
3. Katherine G. Bond, "Living and Dying the Lie," *Teachers in Focus* (Colorado Springs, CO: Focus on the Family, 1998). www.family.org/cforum/teachersmag/a0001037.html
4. Op. Cit. Jones, p. 307.
5. www.medinstitute.org (2003).
6. U.S. Department of Health and Human Services, Health Resources and Services Administration. Section 510 Abstinence Education Grant Program. ftp://ftp.hrsa.gov/mchb/abstinence/statefs.pdf
7. U.S. Department of Health and Human Services, Health Resources and Services Administration. SPRANS Community-based Abstinence Education Project Grant Program. ftp://ftp.hrsa.gov/mchb/abstinence/cbofs.pdf
8. *Guidelines for Comprehensive Sexuality Education: K–12th Grade* (New York and Washington, D.C.:Sexuality Information and Education Council of the United States, 1996).
9. *National Guidelines for Sexuality and Character Education* (Austin, TX: The Medical Institute for Sexual Health, 1996), 33.
10. All About GOD Ministries, Inc., 7150 Campus Drive, Suite 320 Colorado Springs, Colorado 80920 719-884-2246. Website: AllAboutGOD.com and http://www.situational-ethics.com/

Chapter 9 Hot Topics

1. Mark B. Kastleman, *The Drug of the New Millennium: The Science of How Internet Pornography Radically Alters the Human Brain and Body* (Granite Publishing, 2001), 176.
2. Peggy Hartshorn, "Alternatives and Answers to Abortion," *The Salt and Light Solution* (Fort Lauderdale, FL.: Coral Ridge Ministries, 1999).

3. Marian Wallace "The Hidden Link: Abortion and Breast Cancer," *Family Voice,* January 1997.

4. Op. Cit. Hartshorn.

5. Op. Cit. Wallace.

6. "The Legacy of Roe," *Impact,* January 1998.

7. Wayne Brauning, "Should I Keep My Baby?" *Answers to your Kid's Questions,* Chuck Colson, ed. (Wheaton, IL: Tyndale House, 2000).

8. John Frey, *Jesus the Pastor: Leading Others in the Character and Power of Christ* (Grand Rapids: Zondervan Publishing, 2002).

Chapter 10: Handling Teen Pregnancy and Disease

1. National Campaign to Prevent Teen Pregnancy Analysis of S.K. Henshaw (2001). U.S. teenage pregnancy statistics with comparative statistics for women aged 20-24. (New York. The Alan Guttmacher Institute). www.guttmacher.org/pubs/teen_stats.pdf.

2. *Whatever Happened to Childhood? The Problem of Teen Pregnancy in the United States* (Washington, D.C., National Campaign to Prevent Teen Pregnancy, 1997).

3. "National and State-Specific Pregnancy Rates Among Adolescents United States" (Centers for Disease Control and Prevention) MMWR 2000:49 (27): 605–611.

4. M. Males M, K.S. Chew. "The Ages of Fathers in California Adolescent Births, *American Journal of Public Health* 1996 (86, no. 3): 565–568.

5. R.A. Maynard, ed., "Frequently Asked Questions," *Kids Having Kids: A Robin Hood Foundation Special Report on the Costs of Adolescent Childbearing* (New York: Robin Hood Foundation, 1996). www.medinstitute.org.

6. "Sexually Transmitted Disease in America: How Many Cases and at What Cost?" *American Social Health Association* (Menlo Park, CA: Kaiser Family Foundation, 1998).

7. *The Hidden Epidemic: Confronting Sexually Transmitted Disease* (Washington, D.C.: Institute of Medicine, 1997).

8. The Medical Institute, 2003. www.medinstitute.org/medical/faq.htm.

9. Centers for Disease Control and Prevention (1996). Division of STD Surveillance, U.S. Department of Health and Human Services, Public Health Service. Atlanta.

10. "The Nation's Health," *The American Public Health Association* (September 2001).

11. For more information on the Uganda project, see Edward C. Green's prepared witness testimony before the House Committee on Energy and Commerce, March 20, 2003.
    http://energycommerce.house.gov/108/Hearings/03202003.

12. "AIDS Epidemic Update," United Nations Programme on HIV/AIDS. (December 2002). www.unaids.org.

Chapter 11: Consequences and Healing

1   Robert E. Rector, Kirk A. Johnson, Ph.D., and Lauren R. Noyes, "Center for Data Analysis Report #03-04" (June 3, 2003), Heritage Foundation Add Health Study.

2. "Statistics Reveal the Explosion of Teen Suicide." CBN.com, February 27, 2003.

3. Thomas Lickona, "The Neglected Heart: The Emotional Dangers of Premature Sexual Involvement," *American Educator* (Summer 1995): 34–39).

4. *International Standard Bible Encyclopedia, s.v. "sex."*

The Word at Work . . .

*W*hat would you do if you wanted to share God's love with children on the streets of your city? That's the dilemma David C. Cook faced in 1870s Chicago. His answer was to create literature that would capture children's hearts.

Out of those humble beginnings grew a worldwide ministry that has used literature to proclaim God's love and disciple generation after generation. Cook Communications Ministries is committed to personal discipleship—to helping people of all ages learn God's Word, embrace his salvation, walk in his ways, and minister in his name.

Opportunities—and Crisis

We live in a land of plenty—including plenty of Christian literature! But what about the rest of the world? Jesus commanded, "Go and make disciples of all nations" (Matt. 28:19) and we want to obey this commandment. But how does a publishing organization "go" into all the world?

There are five times as many Christians around the world as there are in North America. Christian workers in many of these countries have no more than a New Testament, or perhaps a single shared copy of the Bible, from which to learn and teach.

We are committed to sharing what God has given us with such Christians.

A vital part of Cook Communications Ministries is our international outreach, Cook Communications Ministries International (CCMI). Your purchase of this book, and of other books and Christian-growth products from Cook, enables CCMI to provide Bibles and Christian literature to people in more than 150 languages in 65 countries.

Cook Communications Ministries is a not-for-profit, self-supporting organization. Revenues from sales of our books, Bible curriculum, and other church and home products not only fund our U.S. ministry, but also fund our CCMI ministry around the world. One hundred percent of donations to CCMI go to our international literature programs.

... Around the World

CCMI reaches out internationally in three ways:

· Our premier International Christian Publishing Institute (ICPI) trains leaders from nationally led publishing houses around the world to develop evangelism and discipleship materials to transform lives in their countries.

· We provide literature for pastors, evangelists, and Christian workers in their national language. We provide study helps for pastors and lay leaders in many parts of the world, such as China, India, Cuba, Iran, and Vietnam.

· We reach people at risk—refugees, AIDS victims, street children, and famine victims—with God's Word. CCMI puts literature that shares the Good News into the hands of people at spiritual risk—people who might die before they hear the name of Jesus and are transformed by his love.

Word Power—God's Power

Faith Kidz, RiverOak, Honor, Life Journey, Victor, NexGen — every time you purchase a book produced by Cook Communications Ministries, you not only meet a vital personal need in your life or in the life of someone you love, but you're also a part of ministering to José in Colombia, Humberto in Chile, Gousa in India, or Lidiane in Brazil. You help make it possible for a pastor in China, a child in Peru, or a mother in West Africa to enjoy a life-changing book. And because you helped, children and adults around the world are learning God's Word and walking in his ways.

Thank you for your partnership in helping to disciple the world. May God bless you with the power of his Word in your life.

For more information about our international ministries, visit www.ccmi.org.

Resources for sex education in the image of Christ

Fearless Love: Making Sexual Choices That Honor God

This eight-session study for high schoolers exposes the lies our culture tells about sexual choices and gives students a solid grounding in what God's Word says about sex. The candid lessons provide frank information and equip leaders to truthfully answer the questions youth ask. The study culminates in an opportunity for students to sign a card pledging to be sexually pure and honor God in their sexual choices.

Celebrating Changes:
Everything You Always
Wanted to Know About
Sex in Middle School

Sexuality is a gift from God. But a lot of people are hesitant to talk about it. Kids need the adults around them to give them straight answers. *Celebrating Changes* provides the structure for a one-day seminar for middle school kids and their parents. One option aims at fifth and sixth graders, and another option targets the more sophisticated seventh and eighth graders. The seminar covers the physical changes of puberty as a foundation for talking about godly character in relationships with the opposite sex.

**Visit your local Christian bookstore or
call Cook Communications Ministries
1-800-323-7543
www.cookministries.com**